Lernkrimi Englisch

In the Shadow of the Tower

Barry Hamilton

Compact Verlag

In der Reihe Compact Lernkrimi Classic sind erschienen:
- Englisch, Französisch, Italienisch, Spanisch: B1, B2
- Englisch GB/US, Business English: B1, B2
- Deutsch: B1
- Sammelband Lernkrimi Englisch, Französisch, Spanisch: B1/B2

In der Reihe Compact Lernkrimi Kurzkrimis sind erschienen:
- Englisch, Französisch, Italienisch, Spanisch: A2, B1, Deutsch: A2

In der Reihe Compact Lernkrimi History sind erschienen:
- Englisch: B1, B2, Italienisch: B1

In der Reihe Compact Lernthriller sind erschienen:
- Englisch: B1, B2, Spanisch: B1

In der Reihe Compact Lernstory Mystery sind erschienen:
- Englisch: B1, B2

In der Reihe Compact Lernkrimi Hörbuch sind erschienen:
- Englisch: B1, B2, Business English: B2
- Französisch, Italienisch, Spanisch: B1

In der Reihe Compact Lernkrimi Audio-Learning sind erschienen:
- Englisch: A2, B1, Französisch, Spanisch, Italienisch: B1

In der Reihe Compact Lernkrimi Sprachkurs sind erschienen:
- Englisch, Spanisch: A1/A2

Lernziele:
- Grundwortschatz, Grammatik (A2, B1)
- Aufbauwortschatz, Konversation (B2)

In der Reihe Compact Schüler-Lernkrimi sind erschienen:
- Englisch, Französisch, Spanisch, Latein, Deutsch, Mathematik, Physik, Chemie
- Sammelband Schüler-Lernkrimi Englisch

Weitere Titel sind in Vorbereitung.

© 2010 Compact Verlag GmbH München
Alle Rechte vorbehalten. Nachdruck, auch auszugsweise,
nur mit ausdrücklicher Genehmigung des Verlages gestattet.
Redaktion: Helga Aichele
Fachredaktion: Alison Frankland
Produktion: Wolfram Friedrich
Titelillustration und Stadtplan: Karl Knospe
Typographischer Entwurf: Maria Seidel
Umschlaggestaltung: Carsten Abelbeck

ISBN 978-3-8174-7687-9
7276874

Besuchen Sie uns im Internet: www.compactverlag.de, www.lernkrimi.de

Vorwort

Mit dem neuen, spannenden Compact Lernkrimi können Sie Ihre Englischkenntnisse auf schnelle und einfache Weise vertiefen, auffrischen und überprüfen.

Inspector Hudson erleichtert das Sprachtraining mit Action und Humor. Die Verbrecherjagd führt ihn quer durch London zu vielen Sehenswürdigkeiten.

Der Krimi wird auf jeder Seite durch abwechslungsreiche und kurzweilige Übungen ergänzt, die das Lernen unterhaltsam und spannend machen.

Prüfen Sie Ihr Englisch in Lückentexten, Zuordnungs- und Übersetzungsaufgaben, in Buchstabenspielen und Kreuzworträtseln!

Ob im Bus oder in der Bahn, im Wartezimmer, zu Hause oder in der Mittagspause – das Sprachtraining im handlichen Format bietet die ideale Trainingsmöglichkeit für zwischendurch.

Schreiben Sie die Lösungen einfach ins Buch!

Die richtigen Antworten sind in einem eigenen Lösungsteil am Ende des Buches zusammengefasst. Im Anhang befindet sich außerdem ein Glossar, in dem die schwierigsten Wörter übersetzt sind. Diese sind im Text kursiv markiert.

Und nun kann die Spannung beginnen ...

Viel Spaß und Erfolg!

Die Ereignisse und die handelnden Personen in diesem Buch sind frei erfunden. Etwaige Ähnlichkeiten mit tatsächlichen Ereignissen oder lebenden Personen wären rein zufällig und unbeabsichtigt.

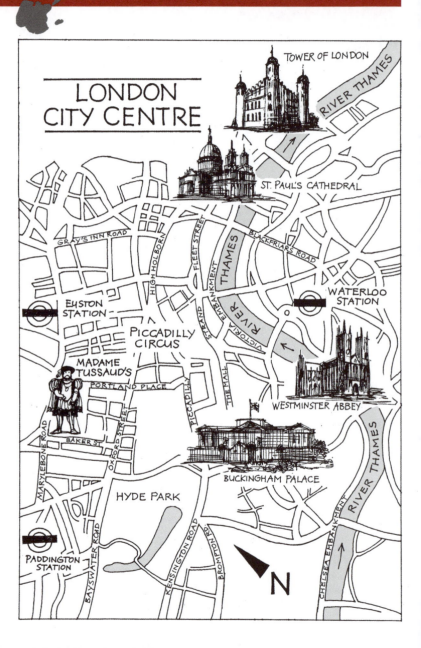

Inhalt

Lernkrimi 6
Abschlusstest 139
Lösungen 143
Glossar 148

Story

James Hudson arbeitet als Inspector bei der legendären Polizeibehörde Scotland Yard. Er ist einer der fähigsten Männer und wird immer dann zu Rate gezogen, wenn seine Kollegen mal wieder vor einem Rätsel stehen. Seine resolute und krimibegeisterte Haushälterin Miss Paddington unterstützt ihn stets mit liebevoller Fürsorge.

Aus dem Tower of London wird der berühmte Diamant „Kohinoor" gestohlen, der Teil der Kronjuwelen ist. Ganz England ist entsetzt. Sir Reginald beauftragt Inspector Hudson mit den Ermittlungen in diesem brisanten Fall, die ihn quer durch London zu vielen Sehenswürdigkeiten führen.
Steckt vielleicht der Wächter Marc Drum, der seit dem Einbruch spurlos verschwunden ist, hinter dem Überfall? Und was führt der mysteriöse indische Prinz im Schilde, der so viel über die Geschichte des Diamanten weiß?

1. The Ceremony of the Keys

At exactly 21:53, the Chief *Yeoman Warder* emerged from the Byward Tower – an outer tower guarding the entrance of the fortress also known as the Tower of London. He was wearing a long red coat and a large round black hat called a Tudor *bonnet*. Mr and Mrs Moore watched with great excitement as the *Beefeater appeared*. They were from York in Northern England and were visiting London for the first time. It had been really difficult for them to get tickets for the ceremony. They had booked three months in advance, and were very pleased to be participating in such an *ancient* tradition.

"Oh, isn't this exciting!" said Mrs Moore to her husband, with a big smile on her face.

Mr Moore nodded, agreeing fully with his wife. In one hand the Chief *Yeoman Warder* was carrying a shining *lantern*, in the other the *Queen's Keys*. He solemnly marched along Water Lane towards *Traitor's Gate*. *Armed foot guards* awaited him there. He *handed* the *lantern* to one of the guards and together they moved on towards the outer gate.

"Did you know that this ceremony has been repeated every night for almost 700 years?"

Mrs Moore looked at her husband in *astonishment*.

"Really!" she exclaimed. "That's amazing!"

"Yes, it was only ever interrupted once during the Second World War."

Mr Moore pointed up to the sky. Mrs Moore looked at her husband with irritation. She looked up to the sky, following his finger.

"*Air raid*!" he said *conspiratorially*.

"Oh!" said Mrs Moore, relieved. "I thought you were going to tell me another one of your alien stories."

Mr Moore shook his head and turned his attention back towards the ceremony. So did his wife. They watched enthusiastically as the guards walked right past them, their steps echoing off the narrow *cobbled* path. As they advanced towards the outer gate, all of the guards and *sentries* saluted the *Queen's Keys*.

"It's a shame you aren't allowed to film or take pictures, isn't it?" said Mr Moore, a note of disappointment in his voice. He looked *longingly* at his camera, which was switched off.

"You could get some really good shots, I tell you."

Mrs Moore *shrugged*, more or less unconcerned by her husband's disappointment. She did not take her eyes off the ceremony.

"There's nothing better than the real thing, that's what I always say," she said.

Übung 1: Wie heißt das Simple Past der folgenden unregelmäßigen Verben?

1. be — was/were
2. get — got
3. go — went
4. hear — heard
5. fall — fell
6. come — came
7. do — did
8. eat — ate
9. let — let
10. say — said

In the meantime, the Chief *Yeoman Warder* had locked the outer gate. He and his escort turned around again. They were *heading back* in the direction they had come from. Mr Moore took his London tourist guide out of his bag and started *flicking through* the pages. Eventually, he found the page he was looking for. Mr

Moore started running his finger along it. Then his finger stopped.
"Ah, do you know what happens now?"
Mrs Moore *tutted*.
"No, but I'm about to find out, am I not?" she said a little annoyed.
Mr Moore sighed and put his book back into his bag. The Chief *Yeoman Warder* marched towards the great *oak* gates. They were located at the Middle Tower. He locked them too.
"Now he just needs to lock the gates at the Byward Tower!" exclaimed Mr Moore excitedly.
Mrs Moore gave her husband an *aggravated* look.
"Could you just hold your breath for five minutes, please, Kevin?"

! Übung 2: *Lesen Sie weiter und setzen Sie die Begriffe in Klammern richtig ein!*
(direction, escort, answer, guard, think, along, archway)

Mr Moore *sulked*. The Chief Warder now returned (1.) _____ Water Lane. He marched towards *Traitor's Gate*. In the shadows of the Bloody Tower (2.) _____, a *sentry* awaited him. Mr Moore's face suddenly lit up again. He was about to say something when his wife said, "Don't even (3.) _____ of it!"

Mr Moore closed his mouth. As soon as the (4.) _____ saw the three men *approach* him, he removed his machine gun from his shoulder. The guard pointed it in their (5.) _____.

He *barked,* "Halt, who comes there?"

The Chief *Yeoman Warder* and his (6.) _____ came to a *stately* halt. "The Keys!" replied the Chief *Yeoman Warder*.

"Whose keys?" asked the guard.

"Queen Elizabeth's Keys," is the (7.) _____ they received.

"Pass Queen Elizabeth's Keys", answered the *sentry*, "and all's well!"

The men were just passing the guard through the so-called Bloody Tower *Archway* when suddenly there was a small explosion. Mr and Mrs Moore and all the other tourists around them jumped. Some murmured and others let out a cry of surprise. The guards also ducked and *took to their guns*. Mr Moore took his tourist guide back out of his bag and nervously started *flicking through* the pages.

"I can't remember reading anything about this!" he remarked.

Then, all of a sudden, there was another explosion. This one was louder and more powerful than the last one. Some people started screaming and shouting. Mr and Mrs Moore *crouched* down.

"What's going on?" Mrs Moore asked her husband *anxiously*.

"I have no idea."

"Lost for an explanation for a change!" said Mrs Moore sarcastically.

Mr Moore had no time to defend himself because white smoke had started to *spread* all around them. Mr and Mrs Moore's eyes began to water and they both began to cough.

"Tear gas!" exclaimed Mr Moore. "We've got to get out of here fast!"

Suddenly, there was a third explosion. This one was even more powerful than the first two together. Everybody started running, screaming and shouting. Mr Moore took his wife by the hand.

"The exit must be over this way somewhere."

By now there was a great *commotion*. People were beginning to panic. They were running all over the place. Every now and again, people *bumped into* Mr and Mrs Moore. Mr Moore decided to turn on his camera.

"What on earth are you doing?" cried Mrs Moore.

"Someone has got to film this," said Mr Moore, *fumbling* with the power *switch*. This was not easy, because he was holding his wife's hand at the same time. He eventually managed to switch it on and held the camera up to his eye.

Through it he could see that some guards were standing at the side of the *cobbled* lane. They were pointing in the direction of the exit.

"Don't panic, now!" one of them said as he waved them past. "Just keep moving. The exit is near."

Another group of guards came rushing past them, their *rifles* pointing out in front of them. Suddenly Mrs Moore stumbled and lost her *grip* on her husband's hand.

"Arghhhh!" she cried out and fell to the ground.

Mr Moore stopped *instantly*. He had to get his wife up fast. There were people behind them already pushing forward. If he did not get his wife up in time, she might be trampled to death. Mr Moore put his camera down and helped his wife to her feet. He was just in time because at that moment, a group of nervously *babbling* Japanese tourists ran by.

"That was close!" breathed Mr Moore heavily.

Mrs Moore smiled gratefully at her husband. They were in a slight state of shock and so just stood still for a moment. The swarm of Japanese tourists seemed to go on forever. One of them stopped and gestured to the Moore's to move on. He was speaking very fast. Then he just shook his head and ran on. Mr and Mrs Moore pulled themselves together again quickly. They had just started to run again, when Mr Moore came to an abrupt halt.

"My camera!" he shouted, pointing back in the direction they had come from. "I need to get my camera back!"

"Forget your camera, Kevin! We need to get out of here fast!" Mrs Moore shouted.

She was *tugging* at his hand, signalling him to move on.

"No, it was very expensive and it's just over there on the ground, I can see it. You run on and I'll catch up with you."

"Oh, well then!" Mrs Moore agreed reluctantly. "You can be so *stubborn* at times, but I'm coming with you."

Übung 3: Übersetzen Sie und enträtseln Sie das Lösungswort!

1. Auto — CAR
2. bewaffnet — ARMED
3. Wache — GUARD
4. Laterne — LANTERN
5. Geld — MONEY
6. schießen — SHOOT
7. enttäuscht — DISAPPOINTED
8. glücklich — HAPPY

Lösung: CEREMONY

Mr and Mrs Moore hurried towards the camera. The smoke was beginning to clear.

"Ah, here it is," said Mr Moore.

Just as he was *bending down* to get it, a man ran past and accidentally kicked it.

"Sorry about that, *mate*!" he shouted as he ran on.

The camera shot along the *cobbled* lane.

"Oh, no!" exclaimed Mr Moore and started running in the direction in which it had been kicked.

"Just leave it, Kevin. Let's just get out of here!"

Mr Moore ignored his wife and kept on walking. Suddenly, huge amounts of smoke started to *spread* around him and a figure dressed all in black *bumped into* him. Mr Moore jumped in fright and looked up in surprise at the person in front of him. He was completely dressed in black. Even his face was covered – *apart from* the sparkling dark eyes staring at him. Mr Moore felt uncomfortable.

"I'm sorry, I was just…"

"Kevin? Kevin, where are you?" Mrs Moore's voice sounded through the clearing smoke. The person in black gave Mr Moore a *piercing* look and disappeared into the smoke. Mr Moore could not believe his eyes as the strange person ran off elegantly, like a *cat of prey*. He was *dumbfounded*. Mrs Moore *appeared*.

"I was worried – I couldn't see you anymore. Where did all that smoke come from? At least it's not tear gas this time," said Mrs Moore, trying in vain to wave the smoke away.

"Did you see that?"

"See what?"

"That mysterious person dressed in black."

"No, I didn't! I think you're beginning to see things," replied Mrs Moore. She *bent down* and picked up the camera.

"No, really…Maybe the *SAS* has arrived."

"*SAS*, Ninja Turtles, whatever. Let's get out of here!"

Mrs Moore gave her husband his camera and they started hurrying back. Mr Moore *inspected* his camera on the way. It seemed to be okay. He started to film again. Mr and Mrs Moore were getting close to the entrance gates.

Übung 4: Finden Sie das passende Gegenteil und setzen Sie die richtige Ziffer ein!

1. hurry
2. shout
3. cover
4. nervous
5. strong
6. keep
7. pull
8. light
9. friend
10. reply

3 uncover
2 calm
7 push
9 enemy
1 slow down
10 ask
5 weak
2 whisper
6 give
5 heavy

"There's Byward Tower!"
Mr Moore pointed at the top of a brown stone building sticking out of the smoke. He moved his camera up to take in the picture. All of a sudden, Mr and Mrs Moore could hear someone shouting:
"Help me, help me! The Keys, someone's taken the *Queen's Keys*!"
The smoke was beginning to clear away again. Mr and Mrs Moore moved in the direction of the voice. They found the Chief *Yeoman Warder* leaning against the wall, holding his *bleeding* head. Mr Moore did not stop filming. Mrs Moore ran over to the man.
"Are you all right?" she asked.
"I'm okay, I'm okay!" he *gasped*. "Someone hit me on the head and took the *Queen's Keys*."

Out of nowhere, guards arrived and helped the Chief Warder to his feet.

"Sir, Madam, please move on!" one of them ordered harshly.

Mr Moore was still filming.

"He ran in that direction!" said the Chief Warder and pointed at Byward Tower.

"Okay, you four secure Byward Tower. I'll escort Mr Drum and these two to the exit. Mr Drum really needs a doctor. I'll be back in a second."

"Yes, sir!" the men shouted. They started running towards Byward Tower.

The guard who stayed behind said to Mr and Mrs Moore: "Now, follow me!"

He noticed Mr Moore was still filming.

"And could you please turn that damn thing off!" he *barked*.

Mr Moore *was startled*.

"Yes, of course…Sorry!" he said, a little *intimidated*.

Übung 5: Welche Adjektive werden gesucht?
(good, clever, helpful, strange, funny, exhausted)

1. The guard was very ___exhausted___.

2. The Chief Warder was ___helpful___.

3. Mr Moore is a very ___good___ filmmaker.

4. The thief was a ___clever___ person.

5. Mrs Moore was not amused; she did not think it was very ___funny___.

6. The Tower was not in a ___good___ condition after the robbery.

The Chief Warder was a little *unsteady* on his feet. The guard put his arm around his shoulders to support him and they all *proceeded* towards the exit. The Chief Warden was still holding his head. Blood was *trickling* over his eyebrow, making it difficult for him to see out of his right eye. Mrs Moore noticed this and took a *handkerchief* out of her bag.
"Here you are, love. Looks quite nasty, that wound of yours."
Mrs Moore *dabbed* it gently and then gave him another *handkerchief* to press against his *bleeding* forehead. Not long after that they reached the Tower's entrance. They crossed the bridge over the *moat*. In the distance, police cars and a couple of ambulances were arriving. There were *flashing* lights everywhere. Two *paramedics* came running towards them. The guard *handed* the Chief Warder over to them.
"Take care of this chap, he is one of our best men!" said the guard.
The *paramedics* took him and started helping him walk towards the ambulance for treatment. They eventually got there.
"Are you both okay?" they asked Mr and Mrs Moore kindly.
"Everything is fine," replied Mr Moore.
Suddenly Mr Moore's knees *gave way* and he would have fallen to the ground if the *paramedic* had not caught him in time. Mrs Moore *started* with fright.
"Kevin!" she exclaimed *anxiously*.
"Was a bit much, eh? All that *commotion* and stuff!" said the *paramedic*, who had caught him, in a sympathetic tone.
"I'm fine, perfectly fine!" Mr Moore protested, *whilst* the *paramedic* helped him to sit down at the back of the ambulance.

However, Mr Moore did look quite pale and so did Mrs Moore.
"Just sit here and wait, we'll be back soon with a hot cup of tea," said one of them.
"Well, that wasn't quite the show we expected," Mrs Moore said after the two men had left.
Her voice was shaky, but Mrs Moore had a weak smile across her face.
Mr and Mrs Moore looked towards the Tower of London. Smoke was still *floating* up into the dark, cloudless sky.
"I certainly hope Buckingham Palace is a bit safer than that place," sighed Mrs Moore.

2. The Jewel House Rock

Inspector Hudson was looking forward to reading the new novel he had just bought at his favourite bookstore. The book was about a man who had emigrated to New Zealand in the late 19th century.

> **!** *Übung 6: Lesen Sie weiter und unterstreichen Sie im folgenden Absatz alle sechs regelmäßigen Verben im Simple Past!*

Inspector Hudson sat on the edge of his bed in his blue and white *striped* pyjamas. He removed his *slippers* and placed them *neatly* to the side, and then he swung his feet onto the bed and covered himself up with the blankets. The inspector *propped up* his pillow, took his book from the bedside table and began to read. He had not been reading long when Miss Paddington knocked on his door. Inspector Hudson frowned; he did not like being disturbed while reading a good book.

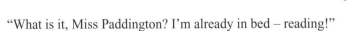

"What is it, Miss Paddington? I'm already in bed – reading!"

"Sorry to disturb you, Mr Hudson, but Sir Reginald is on the phone for you."

"Sir Reginald?"

"Yes!"

Inspector Hudson looked at the clock. It was just after 11 p.m. He sighed.

"Thank you, Miss Paddington, tell him I'll be with him in a minute."

"Will do!" she replied.

Inspector Hudson threw back the covers.

"This can't be good news," he *mumbled* to himself.

Inspector Hudson came down the stairs fully dressed, walked over to the telephone in the hall and picked up the receiver.

"Sir Reginald?"

"Inspector Hudson; at last! We have a national emergency," said Sir Reginald, who sounded extremely worried.

"Why? What's happened?" asked an alarmed Inspector Hudson.

Miss Paddington was standing nearby. She was *pretending* to dust the hall *mantelpiece*, but was actually moving a little closer.

"There has been a robbery at the Tower of London."

"A robbery? You mean to say the Crown Jewels have been stolen?"

Miss Paddington dropped her *duster* and moved right up to Inspector Hudson.

"Not quite. As far as we can tell, only the Kohinoor diamond has been stolen."

"The Kohinoor diamond," said Inspector Hudson thoughtfully. "That's one of the largest diamonds in the world!"

Miss Paddington *was all ears* now. She was trying to get as close to the receiver as she could. She wanted to hear what Sir Reginald was saying, but she *pretended* to dust a vase.

"It's strange, though, that they only took the diamond," said Inspector Hudson, while he tried to move away from Miss Paddington. She was so busy trying to find out exactly what was going on that she did not notice Inspector Hudson move away from her.

"Let us discuss the details when you get here, Inspector, shall we say in half an hour?"

"I'll be there as fast as I can," replied Inspector Hudson.

"Good, see you soon."

"Yes! Goodbye!"

Inspector Hudson put down the phone.

"What's happened?" *inquired* Miss Paddington excitedly.

"I'm not fully *in the picture*; however, someone *appears* to have stolen the Kohinoor diamond from the Tower of London."

"Oh, dear!" exclaimed Miss Paddington, putting her hand to her mouth. "That is *dreadful*. Has anybody been hurt?"

"I don't know. I'll soon find that out too."

Inspector Hudson put on his coat and hurried towards the door.

"Mr Hudson!" Miss Paddington shouted. "You still have your *slippers* on."

Inspector Hudson looked down at his feet.

"Oh, so I have," he laughed.

Miss Paddington hurried over with his shoes; he put them on and rushed back to the door.

"*Keep me posted*," shouted Miss Paddington to the inspector as he was closing the door behind him.

Übung 7: Beantworten Sie folgende Fragen im Simple Past!

1. What did Inspector Hudson look forward to?

2. What did Inspector Hudson wear while he sat on his bed?

_____

3. What did the thieves steal?

_____

4. What did Miss Paddington try to do while Inspector Hudson talked to Sir Reginald?

_____

5. What did Inspector Hudson forget to put on?

_____

Inspector Hudson walked *swiftly* towards the Tower of London. He passed ambulances and police cars – their lights shooting red and blue rays into the dark London sky. The inspector walked past people with blankets around their shoulders, drinking hot tea. Some of them were talking to the police; others were having *minor* wounds treated. Sir Reginald was standing near the entrance of the Tower. He was talking to a group of police officers. He looked up and saw Inspector Hudson *approaching*. Sir Reginald excused himself and hurried in the inspector's direction. They met and shook hands.

Übung 8: Welches Wort ist das „schwarze Schaf"? Unterstreichen Sie das nicht in die Reihe passende Wort!

1. anybody, somebody, nobody, someone
2. I, you, his, they
3. looked, frowned, sat, disturbed

4. dark, dim, bright, gloomy
5. say, think, speak, talk
6. far, near, close, next to
7. wound, blood, scar, cut
8. paramedic, doctor, ambulance, nurse
9. shoes, slippers, boots, socks
10. immediately, later, instantly, directly

"Inspector Hudson, thank you for coming so quickly," he said *firmly*. "It's probably best we *proceed* to the crime scene *straight away*."

The two men started walking towards the Tower.

"What exactly happened?" asked Inspector Hudson.

"We are not quite sure. All we know for certain is what I have already mentioned. Someone broke into the Jewel House and stole the Kohinoor diamond. It all happened during the *Ceremony of the Keys*. The thieves used smoke bombs and tear gas to create a *diversion* – the whole place was in an uproar."

"Thieves?" *inquired* Inspector Hudson. "Do you know for sure it was more than one person?"

"We are not sure. However, do you really believe someone could have *pulled* this *off* by himself?"

"Stranger things have happened," said Inspector Hudson with a philosophical undertone.

"Did anybody see them?"

"Well, yes and no," replied Sir Reginald. "Our main *witness* has disappeared into thin air. The Chief *Yeoman Warder*, Marc Drum, was knocked *unconscious* and the *Queen's Keys* were stolen from him. The thieves used them to *make* their *way* into the Jewel House."

"Disappeared? When was he last seen?"

"He was being treated outside the Tower *premises*. After his head was bandaged, he *vanished*."

"That's very strange," said Inspector Hudson thoughtfully.

"Do we know what he saw?"

"All we know just now is that he was knocked *unconscious* and then the *Queen's Keys* were taken from him."

"But why would he disappear?"

"Nobody knows. The *paramedics* think it could be post-traumatic shock or something like that. I have men out there looking for him."

"You don't think he could…?" asked Inspector Hudson carefully.

"Certainly not, Inspector! Mr Drum is a very *honourable* man – he has *bravery* awards and has achieved everything a man of honour can accomplish."

Inspector Hudson *shrugged*, "It was just a thought. And anyway, what does that mean, 'Man of Honour' – a very rare *species* if you ask me."

Sir Reginald was just going to say something back when Inspector Hudson *wisely* changed the subject.

"Are there any other *witnesses*?" he asked.

"Yes, a Mr and Mrs Moore from York. Mr Moore says he *collided* with one of the thieves."

"Did he see who it was?"

"No, he only saw the *intruder's* eyes. *Apart from* that, the thief was dressed in black – from head to toe. We have asked him to come round to the station tomorrow. He was a bit *shaken*, so we sent him and his wife home. They are staying at a hotel on Piccadilly Circus."

By this time the two policemen had reached the Jewel House, which is located inside the Tower in the so-called Waterloo *Barracks*. They entered.

Übung 9: Vervollständigen Sie die Sätze, wenn nötig, mit den Artikeln *a*, *an* oder *the*!

1. Inspector Hudson travelled by ___/___ car.
2. __The__ Kohinoor diamond was stolen.
3. The guards made __a__ big mistake.
4. The robbery happened half __an__ hour ago.
5. Inspector Hudson got back out of __~~the~~/__ bed.
6. Mr Moore collided with one of __the__ thieves.
7. If caught, the thieves will have to go to ___/___ prison.
8. The Jewel House is inside __the__ Tower.

"This is so much bigger than I remember it," said an impressed Inspector Hudson.

The whole ground floor of the Waterloo *Barracks* was taken up by the Crown Jewels. They were shining and *sparkling* in their *see-through* glass boxes – resting peacefully on French *velvet*.

"The Jewel House was newly constructed between 1991 and 1994," said Sir Reginald. "The display area is three times the size of the old Jewel House – the room *is capable of* handling up to 2,500 visitors an hour." Sir Reginald nodded intently at Inspector Hudson.

"That is very *impressive*," said Inspector Hudson, who was almost *spellbound* by the *riches* around him – something that did not happen very often to Inspector Hudson.

Sir Reginald saw this and smiled. Inspector Hudson noticed this and felt a little embarrassed. He cleared his throat:

"But they could have invested a little more in security!" exclaimed the inspector. He tried to sound *matter-of-factly*.

"There is nothing wrong with being impressed, Inspector. I mean, you are standing in front of one of the most exclusive collections of jewels in the world."

Inspector Hudson just *grunted*.

"Where was the Kohinoor diamond kept?" he asked, changing the subject.

"Over there!"

Sir Reginald pointed to the other end of the room, where a group of policemen were busy securing *evidence*. The policemen walked towards the glass case which used to contain the Kohinoor diamond. As Sir Reginald led the way to the case, Inspector Hudson could not help admiring the Crown Jewels they passed on their way. He saw the *Sceptre* with the Cross – its diamond shining in the light, almost blinding him. He also admired the three *swords*: The *Sword* of *Spiritual Justice*, the *Sword* of *Temporal Justice*, and the *Sword* of *Mercy*. The latter has a *blunt* point because it is a symbolically broken *sword*. Sir Reginald turned around slightly and again saw the astounded look on Inspector Hudson's face. He smiled triumphantly.

"The legend says that the *Sword* of *Mercy's* tip was broken off by an angel to prevent a *wrongful* killing."

"Oh really!" replied Inspector Hudson, trying hard not to show too much interest.

Sir Reginald and Inspector Hudson eventually reached the empty case where the Kohinoor diamond had been kept. They could clearly see where a circle had been cut out – large enough for a hand and the diamond to fit through.

"Clean cut," remarked Inspector Hudson. "The thieves seem to have been well *equipped*."

"Yes, it's not easy to open one of these cases. The jewels are protected by two inch-thick *shatter-proof* glass."

Inspector Hudson nodded thoughtfully.

"The thieves must have used a special kind of machinery, possibly even a diamond to open the case. They were obviously very well organized and very competent – it's certainly not *philistines* we are dealing with."

"No, that's for sure," agreed Sir Reginald.

"And the fact that almost nobody saw them; so many people and only two *witnesses*."

"There was a lot of smoke and tourists were running around *frantically* – it was chaos, total chaos."

"It's strange that none of the guards saw anything. Did they not secure the Jewel House *straight away*?" asked Inspector Hudson *incredulously*.

"Well, the thing was that most of the guards ran towards Byward Tower."

"But that's more or less in the opposite direction from the Jewel House," stated Inspector Hudson. "Why did they do that?"

"Marc Drum, the Chief *Yeoman Warder*, told them the thief who *struck* him *down* had run in that direction."

"Did he now?" asked Inspector Hudson suspiciously.

"It was probably due to the blow on the head. I mean the man was quite obviously disorientated," Sir Reginald fired back.

"Yes, maybe," Inspector Hudson said, more to himself.

Inspector Hudson looked *pensively* around the room. He looked up at the cameras staring down on them.

"Do we have anything on film?" he asked.

Sir Reginald *shrugged*.

"I have not found that out yet."

"Where is the control room where the soldiers monitor the Jewel House?"

"It's also in the *barracks*."

Übung 10: Übersetzen Sie die folgenden Sätze!

1. Das ist sehr beeindruckend.

2. Sie gingen auf die Vitrine zu.

3. Inspector Hudson bewunderte die Juwelen.

4. Sir Reginald lächelte triumphierend.

5. Es gab fast keine Zeugen.

6. Inspector Hudson sah sich nachdenklich im Zimmer um.

7. Sir Reginald zuckte mit den Schultern.

Inspector Hudson turned around to the policemen who were securing the crime scene. One of them was busily scanning the broken case with an ultraviolet light.

"Sergeant Wood, have your men checked the film material yet?" asked Inspector Hudson.

Sergeant Wood looked up at the Inspector. He did not stop what he was doing.

"Yes, I'm afraid we have nothing," he said with a sigh. Sergeant

Wood *carried on* with his work. "One of the thieves managed to get into the control room and take out the cassettes."

"But where were the guards?" asked an astonished Sir Reginald.

"They were all running towards Byward Tower," answered Sergeant Wood dryly. "The two that stayed behind were *stunned* by electroshock guns."

"And none of them saw the thief or thieves either?" asked Inspector Hudson, a little frustrated.

"*Nope*!" Sergeant Wood looked up from his work. A guard had just entered the room. The three of them looked in his direction.

"You can ask Mr Gunn. He was one of the guards who were *stunned*."

Übung 11: Setzen Sie die richtigen Fragepronomen ein! (who, whose, which (2x), why, where, what)

1. _____ does the Kohinoor diamond originally come from?
2. In _____ part of the Tower was the diamond stolen?
3. _____ happened to the Chief Yeoman Warder?
4. _____ was one of the stunned guards?
5. _____ sword is that?
6. _____ room did the thief manage to get into?
7. _____ did they steal only one diamond?

Inspector Hudson and Sir Reginald walked towards the guard. He was still wearing his traditional *Beefeater* uniform called the blue undress uniform – it was dark blue in colour and *emblazoned* with red *trimmings*. His face was rather pale and he was not wearing his Tudor *bonnet*. The policemen introduced themselves to the *Beefeater*. He returned their greeting tiredly.

"It's a very sad day for us *Yeoman Warders*, a nightmare come true," said Mr Gunn, *gloomily* shaking his head.

Sir Reginald and Inspector Hudson looked at him sympathetically. "Sergeant Wood told us you were attacked?"

"Yes, we had no chance. The thief came out of nowhere…Like in some Batman film…I didn't even have time to turn round. Before I knew it I felt this terrible pain *rack* my body – that's the last thing I remember," said Mr Gunn dully.

"And your colleague?" asked Inspector Hudson.

"Nothing, he dropped to the ground before I did…It was terrible…I never thought…We totally failed…"

Mr Gunn's voice broke.

"Now, now!" said Sir Reginald clapping the man on the back. "You did the best you could."

Mr Gunn smiled *wearily*.

"Whatever you say; I guess the other men and I will have to live with this failure somehow. I hope to God you get them. That would at least be a small comfort."

"We'll do our best," replied Inspector Hudson.

"I hope you do better than us," said Mr Gunn and with this he left the room, his shoulders and head hanging low.

"Poor soul," said Sir Reginald *compassionately* as he watched the *Beefeater* leave.

"I should get back to the police station. For all I know, the Queen herself could be waiting in my office to find out what exactly has happened," he said worriedly.

"This whole affair is going to be all over the newspapers tomorrow! We need some answers, we need some answers fast!"

"I'll do my best, Sir," Inspector Hudson assured him. "Let me *accompany* you back outside. I could do with some fresh air."

> **Übung 12:** *Lesen Sie weiter und ordnen Sie die Buchstaben in Klammern zu einem sinnvollen Wort!*

The two policemen (1. xetied) _____ the Jewel House. Sir Reginald and Inspector Hudson (2. dlkeaw) _____ over to the *moat* bridge. Inspector Hudson took a deep breath and *inhaled* the fresh night air.

"I wonder why they just stole the Kohinoor (3. nomadid) _____; I mean they could have taken the lot? What is so (4. icaleps) _____ about it?"

Sir Reginald (5. shggedur) _____ slightly and said thoughtfully: "No idea!"

At that moment a red car suddenly (6. eepsedd) _____ around the corner and came to a sudden halt. The two policemen looked over to the road to see what was going on. Sir Reginald smiled. Inspector Hudson did not look (7. pldeeas) _____.

"However, maybe Miss Elliot can help you on that one, Inspector Hudson," said Sir Reginald with a tone of amusement in his voice as he watched Elvira Elliot – a young and attractive insurance *investigator* – walk quickly but elegantly towards them – her long red hair flying through the air like the trail of a *blazing* comet.

3. An Absent Husband

The next day, Inspector Hudson and Elvira Elliot decided to visit the wife of the missing *Beefeater*, Marc Drum. The Drums lived in the *outskirts* of London, in Barnet.

Elvira Elliot was driving her fire-red sports car round a bend at speed, Inspector Hudson was holding on to the *dashboard*. He was trying very hard not to fall into Miss Elliot's lap.

The road straightened up.

Inspector Hudson relaxed.

Elvira turned to face him and smiled.

"It's strange that Marc Drum is still missing, isn't it?" she said conversationally.

"Yes, very strange, suspiciously strange," he replied.

Elvira Elliot was still looking at the inspector. He nodded in the direction of the road.

"Maybe you should keep an eye on the road," he said worriedly.

Miss Elliot turned her attention back to the road and asked:

"You're not frightened, are you, Inspector?" She smiled *pensively*.

"No, I'm not frightened; just cautious," Inspector Hudson answered calmly.

They shot round another bend. The inspector grasped the *dashboard* again.

"That's us nearly there, not far to go now," Miss Elliot grinned.

"What do you know about the Kohinoor diamond?" the inspector asked, looking at Miss Elliot.

Übung 13: Fügen Sie die richtige Präposition ein!
(onto, in, under, on (2x), over, to)

1. The sword lay _____ a silk cushion.

2. Elvira Elliot walked _____ to them.

3. Inspector Hudson and Miss Elliot were _____ her red sports car.

4. The red sports car was _____ the road.

5. As she drove round the bend, the inspector was close _____ her.

6. Elvira Elliot drove _____ a bridge.

7. Inspector Hudson nearly fell _____ Miss Elliot's lap.

Elvira Elliot turned and faced him again. Inspector Hudson pointed in the direction of the road. Miss Elliot faced the road again.
"It's the oldest diamond known to *mankind*…"
"Approximately five thousand years old," interrupted Inspector Hudson.
"Oh, I'm impressed. I see you've done your homework. Anyway, it's one of the largest diamonds in the world and the legend says that whoever carries it in their crown shall rule the world."
"Does it? It's amazing how many legends and secrets are attached to all these jewels."
"Yes, it's a diamond which has never been bought or sold, but it has *changed hands* many times. The diamond has left a trail of *greed*, power, murder, *misfortune* and unhappiness behind it."
"Oh, dear, then the thief is in big trouble!" Inspector Hudson said ironically.
"Yes, he is indeed – especially after we get him," she laughed.

"How much is the diamond worth?" the inspector asked.
"That's very difficult to say. It has 105 carats, which is rather a lot. Plus you have the, how shall I put it, sentimental value. I guess it goes into millions."
Inspector Hudson *whistled*.

Übung 14: Welches Wort hat die stärkere Bedeutung? Kreuzen Sie an!

1. ☐ trouble   ☐ danger
2. ☐ miserable ☐ unhappy
3. ☐ difficult ☐ thorny
4. ☐ alert   ☐ cautious
5. ☐ much   ☐ loads
6. ☐ argue   ☐ disagree
7. ☐ greed   ☐ excess

"So it wouldn't make much sense to cut the diamond into pieces?"
"Not really."
"But is that not stupid? I mean, it won't be easy to sell because of its fame."
"Yes and no. Countries such as Pakistan and India have often claimed to be the *rightful* owners of the diamond."
"That means you just need the right connections."
"Yes, you need to know the right people. But as you know, this is all speculation."
"I guess you're right there, for all we know the thief might just want to put the diamond on his living room *mantelpiece*."
Miss Elliot and Inspector Hudson laughed.
"There is one other thing that's annoying me," the inspector said.

"And what might that be?"

"Why was the Kohinoor diamond stolen? There were much more *valuable treasures* in the Jewel House. The 'Great Star of Africa', for example – it has 530 carats."

Elvira Elliot *shrugged*. "As I pointed out, the Kohinoor diamond has a special *reputation*."

Inspector Hudson nodded. "We should keep that in mind. It is a very good point, Miss Elliot."

Elvira Elliot smiled.

"Oh, here we are!" exclaimed Elvira Elliot, suddenly hitting the brakes.

The car came to an abrupt halt. Inspector Hudson flew forward.

"Sorry about that!" she apologized. "But we nearly drove past Mr and Mrs Drum's house."

Inspector Hudson just looked at her *disapprovingly* and got out of the car.

! Übung 15: Geben Sie die verneinte Form in ihrer Kurzform an!

1. he is   he isn't
2. they are   _____
3. we will   _____
4. she did   _____
5. it can   _____
6. she would   _____
7. we have   _____
8. they should   _____

The *investigators* walked towards the house and rang the bell. A young woman in her early thirties opened the door. She looked pale and worried. Inspector Hudson and Miss Elliot introduced themselves. Mrs Drum let them in and led them to her living room.

"Please take a seat," Mrs Drum said nervously.

Miss Elliot and the inspector sat down.

"Can I offer you a cup of tea?" Mrs Drum asked.

Inspector Hudson and Miss Elliot *declined*.

Mrs Drum sat down on the armchair opposite them.

"Have you heard anything?" she *inquired anxiously*.

"No, I'm afraid not. Your husband has disappeared into thin air," the inspector replied.

Mrs Drum played around uneasily with her hands. Then she put a hand to her eyes and started to cry.

"It's all so *dreadful*. I'm so worried about him. And these journalists…", Mrs Drum pointed at her phone which she had taken off the hook, "…they have not stopped calling all morning," she sobbed.

"I suspect your husband has not *been in touch* with you either?" Miss Elliot asked cautiously.

Mrs Drum shook her head. She took a *handkerchief* out of her pocket and blew her nose.

"Do you also believe he has something to do with the robbery?" she asked sadly.

"We can't say for sure, but to be honest, Mrs Drum, he is one of our main *suspects* at the moment," replied Inspector Hudson.

Mrs Drum started to cry again. She could not stop. Elvira Elliot went over to her and tried to calm her down. She *stroked* her back gently.

"Now, now Mrs Drum, there might be a harmless explanation for his disappearance."

"Yes, it might be shock. My men are out there looking for him," the inspector said.

Mrs Drum started to calm down. She blew her nose again.

"I understand your worry", Inspector Hudson *carried on,* "but I need you to answer some questions."

Mrs Drum nodded.

"What would you like to know, Inspector?"

"When was the last time you saw your husband?" Inspector Hudson asked.

"Yesterday evening around five o'clock before he went to the Tower."

"Did he act strangely in any way?"

"No, everything was the same as usual."

"Did he seem nervous or *distracted*?"

"No, not really," Mrs Drum thought for a short moment. "But come to think of it, he received a phone call just before he left. After that he did seem somewhat nervous."

> **Übung 16:** *Lesen Sie weiter und unterstreichen Sie jeweils die richtige Variante!*

"Do you know who (1.) named/called?"

"No!"

"(2.) Him/He didn't say anything about the phone call?" Inspector Hudson *inquired*.

"I'm afraid not, Inspector. Perhaps (3.) me/I am overestimating its relevance – maybe he just lost a bet."

"A bet?" the inspector asked (4.) interestedly/interested.

"Yes, that does happen sometimes."

"Did your husband bet a lot?"

"No, not really. He just puts the *odd* one on now and again."
"So you had (5.) no/know money problems or anything?"
"What are you trying to (6.) tell/say, Inspector? Do you think my husband stole the Kohinoor diamond to pay off his *gambling debts*?" Mrs Drum asked annoyed.
"(7.) Came/Calm down Mrs Drum," said Miss Elliot. "Inspector Hudson is only (8.) doing/making his job."

"Yes, I'm sorry. I guess I'm a little *worked up*."
Inspector Hudson took a deep breath and *carried on*.
"*Apart from* the incident yesterday evening, Mrs Drum, is there anything else you can think of?"
Mrs Drum had another good think.
"Well, to be honest there was. During the last few months he often came home late and the *secretive* phone call last night was not the first."
"Why didn't you say so in the first place?" Elvira Elliot asked pointedly.
"I was a little embarrassed to talk about it." Mrs Drum ran her fingers through her hair nervously.
"Why is that?" *inquired* the inspector.
"Well you see…How shall I put it…I believe my husband is having an affair."
"What makes you think that?" Inspector Hudson asked.
Mrs Drum looked at Elvira Elliot. Her face looked sad.
"Just one of these female intuition things, if you know what I mean."
Elvira Elliot nodded understandingly.
"I see, so you have no proof?"
"No, Inspector, I have no proof. Nor can I prove my husband is innocent – but I do feel he is."

Übung 17: Welche Synonyme gehören zusammen? Setzen Sie die richtige Ziffer ein!

1. ask
2. innocent
3. exclaim
4. close
5. accomplice
6. pull
7. understand
8. force
9. proceed
10. rough

- [ ] advance
- [ ] heave
- [ ] comprehend
- [ ] inquire
- [ ] violent
- [ ] shout
- [ ] blameless
- [ ] shut
- [ ] assistant
- [ ] might

Mrs Drum started to cry again. Elvira Elliot comforted her.

Suddenly a bright *flash* came from outside the living room window.

"What on earth was that?" exclaimed Miss Elliot, who was nearly blinded by the light.

Inspector Hudson ran to the window. He saw a man with a camera and a film crew.

"Journalists!" he exclaimed.

Elvira Elliot went to the window too. She looked out.

"It certainly is!" she remarked. A cameraman pointed the camera in her direction.

Inspector Hudson closed the *blinds*.

"I'll see to them!" he *snarled*.

Inspector Hudson opened the front door.

"Okay, you lot. Make a move!"

A presenter recognized the inspector *straight away* and moved towards him. He was followed by a camera. He stuck his microphone right in James Hudson's face.

"So what have you found out, Inspector? Have you caught the *Beefeater* Marc Drum yet?"

"I said, clear off! This is *trespassing*!" Inspector Hudson said harshly.

The reporter did not move.

"Did he *pull off* the robbery on his own or did he have *accomplices*?"

"No comment!" answered the inspector. And with that he started to push the cameraman and the reporter back. He put his hand over the lens of the camera.

"What are you doing?" cried the news reporter. "You can't do this!"

"Oh, yes I can!" Inspector Hudson answered as he forced them back onto the pavement outside the Drums' property.

"Now you can stand here all you want, but I don't want to see you anywhere near that window. Do you understand? Or I'll have you all arrested."

The man with the photo camera took a picture of the *enraged* inspector, who was already walking back to the front door. He went inside, locked it and then walked back into the living room.

"That was a bit rough, wasn't it?" Elvira Elliot remarked.

Inspector Hudson *shrugged* unconcernedly.

"Is that all you can do, Inspector? Can you not ban them from my street?"

"I'm afraid not, Mrs Drum. As much as I'd like to, that's all I can do for now."

Mrs Drum was very upset and *distressed*.

"What a scandal. The whole affair is going to be splattered all over tomorrow's newspapers and poor Marc is just *fodder* for their *sensation-craving* readers. And…"

Inspector Hudson cleared his throat. Mrs Drum stopped talking.

"If you don't mind, Miss Elliot and I would like to have a look around your house – and especially search your husband's *belongings* for any *clues*. Would you mind?"

"Not at all. The sooner you prove his innocence the better. If you follow me, I'll show you his little office. That's where he spends most of his free time."

*Übung 18: Setzen Sie **many** oder **much** richtig ein!*

1. Inspector Hudson didn't have _____ time to solve the case.
2. Mrs Drum could not tell them very _____ about her husband's motive.
3. Marc Drum had _____ friends.
4. There were not _____ reasons why Mr Drum could have disappeared.
5. The Beefeater spent _____ of his time in his office.
6. There are not _____ clues.

Mrs Drum took the *investigators* along the hall and led them into a small office. It had two full bookshelves and a desk with a *typewriter*.

"Does your husband not have a computer?" Miss Elliot asked.

"No!" answered Mrs Drum. "He is more of an old-fashioned type." Mrs Drum left them to it.

"Well, what would you expect of a *Beefeater*," Elvira Elliot remarked. "He runs around with a large fork in his hand all day." Inspector Hudson smiled.

"Let's get to work, see if we can find anything that might help us solve Drum's mysterious disappearance."

Übung 19: Verwandeln Sie das Adjektiv in ein Adverb!

1. gentle
2. thoughtful
3. uneasy
4. harmless
5. safe
6. rough
7. abrupt
8. mysterious

After searching for a while, Elvira Elliot found a card from the Savoy Hotel, a *renowned* London luxury hotel. She turned it over. On the back it had a time and date: "16.07. 8 p.m."
"Look at this," she said and *handed* the card to Inspector Hudson. "Strange, isn't it?"
"Yes, it is."
"Why would a man like Marc Drum have an appointment at that kind of luxury hotel?"
"Good question. Perhaps we should go there and find out. It could well be that somebody saw him there."
"Yes, good idea. Hotel receptions and *bellboys* are often the best informants."
Miss Elliot and Inspector Hudson left Mr Drum's office.

Übung 20: *Sind die folgenden Aussagen richtig? Markieren Sie mit richtig ✔ oder falsch – !*

1. Mrs Drum couldn't care less if her husband were dead or alive.
2. Marc Drum has a very modern computer.
3. Inspector Hudson and Miss Elliot look around the house.
4. Marc Drum is old-fashioned.
5. Elvira Elliot found a fax from the Savoy Hotel.
6. The Savoy Hotel is very expensive.
7. The inspector and Miss Elliot plan to go to the Savoy.

Miss Elliot and Inspector Hudson arrived at the Savoy Hotel. It is located in a very famous street in London called "Strand". The Strand, as the street is also referred to, starts at Trafalgar Square and runs east to the *boundary* of the City of London, where it becomes Fleet Street. Elvira Elliot stopped her car right in front of the entrance. A *bellboy* walked *swiftly* towards the car. He was no older than seventeen.

"Did we need the *grand entrance*?" Inspector Hudson asked, irritated. "We could have just parked on the street!"

Elvira Elliot was fixing her hair in the *rear-view mirror*.

"Why shouldn't we take a little luxury when we can get it?" she smiled.

The *bellboy* opened Inspector Hudson's door.

"Good day, sir!" he said.

Inspector Hudson did not really like this special attention. He sighed and got out of the car.

"Well, yes, a good day to you too, young man," the inspector said, slightly unsure of himself.

The *bellboy* thought this reaction a little strange and walked around to the other side of the car. He opened the door and let Miss Elliot out. She slid elegantly out of the car.

"Good day, Madam!"

"Good day!"

Elvira Elliot *handed* him the keys and smiled. The *bellboy* took them from her, got in the car and drove it away.

"I hope you get it back!" remarked Inspector Hudson. "For all we know he's planning on having a *joyride* through London."

Miss Elliot laughed. They walked into the hotel.

Übung 21: Ergänzen Sie die fehlenden Verbformen!

	Infinitive	Simple Past	Past Participle
1.	arrive		
2.			run
3.		hid	
4.	make		
5.			kept
6.		shone	
7.	think		
8.			worn

The reception area was *vast*. The hotel first opened in 1889 and still had a unique *Victorian* touch. Although very exquisite, the Savoy had a warm and friendly atmosphere. Inspector Hudson and Miss Elliot *made* their *way* to the reception. The inspector took out his *badge* and showed it to one of the receptionists. The two *investigators* introduced themselves. The receptionist did not seem very impressed. He *carried on flicking through* some letters.

Übung 22: Welche Wörter gehören zusammen? Bilden Sie zusammengesetzte Begriffe!

1. boy
2. joy
3. lobby
4. badge
5. book
6. fashioned
7. writer

- [ ] hotel
- [ ] police
- [ ] bell
- [ ] old
- [ ] type
- [ ] ride
- [ ] shelf

"How may I help you?"
Elvira Elliot lay down a photograph of Marc Drum.
"Have you ever seen this man?" she asked.
The receptionist *glanced* at it.
"I've never seen him," he replied.
The receptionist *carried on* sorting the letters. Miss Elliot and Inspector Hudson looked at each other. Elvira Elliot just shook her head. They also asked the other receptionists; however, nobody recognized Marc Drum. The *investigators* walked away from the reception.
"That was not very successful, was it?" Inspector Hudson said dryly. "They've all got their noses too high in the air here if you ask me."
Elvira Elliot *shrugged* and said excitedly, "I like the Savoy!"
The insurance *investigator* looked around, her eyes *sparkling* with

joy. Inspector Hudson *frowned* and shook his head.
"Do you come here often?" he asked *mockingly*.
"No, but I would if I could afford it!"

4. The Stunning Prince

Elvira Elliot and the inspector were just about to leave the hotel when a little blond woman came hurrying up behind them. She was wearing the same uniform as the other receptionists. The young woman looked to the left and then to the right. It was as if she wanted to check she was not being watched.

Übung 23: Das englische Wort hat verschiedene Übersetzungsmöglichkeiten. Welche?

1. watch
2. uniform
3. ring
4. hand
5. mine
6. muse

"Can I see that photograph again, please?" she asked.
Inspector Hudson showed it to her.
"Have you seen this man here?" Inspector Hudson *inquired*.
The woman looked at the photograph; she bit on her lip.
"Yes, I think so."

"When?" the inspector wanted to know.

"It must have been about a week ago. He was sitting in the tea room talking to an Indian gentleman."

"Do you know who this Indian gentleman was?" the inspector asked with great interest.

"Yes, his name is Prince Vikram."

"Is he…"

The woman interrupted Inspector Hudson.

"That's all I know. I must get back to work."

The receptionist walked away *swiftly*.

"Now isn't that interesting? Marc Drum meeting up with an Indian prince," Miss Elliot stated.

"Yes, it is rather strange. Why should a wealthy Indian prince meet up with an English working-class *Beefeater*?"

In that moment the *bellboy* walked by. It was the same one who had parked Elvira's car.

Übung 24: Setzen Sie die passenden Synonyme ein!
(eagerly, point, waved, generous, approached, inquired, usual)

Miss Elliot *caught* his *eye* and (1. gestured) _____ him over. He smiled and (2. moved towards) _____ her. She smiled *flirtatiously* at him.

"Do you *by any chance* know who Prince Vikram is?" she (3. asked) _____.

"Everybody knows Prince Vikram! He's a very (4. charitable) _____ man."

Then he *bent* over and whispered into Miss Elliot's ear, "Like most people who come in here."

The *bellboy* nodded *conspiratorially*. Then he moved back and said in his (5. normal) _____ voice, "So what do you want to know?"

Miss Elliot got the (6. message) _____ and took out her purse. She held it in her hand.

"Do you happen to know where the prince is just now?" she asked.

The *bellboy* looked (7. enthusiastically) _____ at the purse.

"Well, he's not at the hotel at the moment, but I *overheard* a conversation earlier on."
"Regarding what?" the inspector asked.
"Prince Vikram was planning a tour of London today. His first destination was St. Paul's Cathedral."
"When did he leave?" Miss Elliot asked.
The *bellboy* looked at his watch.
"About half an hour ago."
"What does he actually look like, this prince?" Inspector Hudson asked.
"You can't really miss him; he wears a white turban with a large shiny *scarlet gem* stuck on the front."
Elvira Elliot *handed* the *bellboy* ten pounds.
"Thank you for your assistance!" she said.
The *bellboy* just looked at the money as if to say: Is that all?
Miss Elliot sighed and shook her head.

"You are very *demanding* nowadays, you young people."
She reluctantly gave him another ten.
"Thank you, Madam!" he smiled.
"Don't Madam me, just get my car!" Miss Elliot exclaimed.
Inspector Hudson could not help laughing – *affectionately* amused by Elvira Elliot's sudden *objection* to *snobbishness*.

Übung 25: Wie lauten die Sätze? Achten Sie auf die Wortstellung!

1. always fast Miss drives Elliot

_____

2. she saw suddenly the bellboy

_____

3. the Inspector Hudson into Elvira Elliot walked and just hotel

_____

4. just already Prince Vikram left had

_____

5. first Inspector Hudson asked the should probably have bellboy

_____

Elvira Elliot was *speeding* along Fleet Street.
"It's not far to St. Paul's Cathedral. The cathedral is on Ludgate Hill; and at some point Fleet Street in fact becomes Ludgate Hill. We should be there *in no time*," Miss Elliot said.
"Yes, if we actually get there alive!" *mumbled* Inspector Hudson.
Shortly after Miss Elliot's race down Fleet Street, they arrived at St.

Paul's Cathedral. Elvira Elliot parked the car and the *investigators* walked quickly towards the cathedral.

Übung 26: Lesen Sie weiter und unterstreichen Sie die fünf inhaltlich nicht dazugehörenden Sätze!

They entered the cathedral, which lies to the east of the so-called Great West Door. They walked outside. Being one of London's most visited sites, it was quite busy. Some people were *strolling* up the *nave* – the main *approach* leading to the high altar. They were admiring the cathedral's architecture, which was constructed in late Renaissance style. It was a very modern building. The visitors were obviously *spellbound* by the Cathedral's *seemingly eternal* vastness. Some of them were seated along the *aisles* praying or just *marvelling at* the spectacular *dome*. It was inspired by St. Peter's Basilica in Rome and rose up to 108 metres. It was a very cheap copy. Inspector Hudson and Elvira Elliot walked up the *nave*. They could see land in the distance. The *pillars* on both sides, like colossal fingers reaching out to heaven, held the gigantic roof in place. The whole *interior* of St. Paul's Cathedral was mainly greyish-white in colour. It was like a rainbow. It reflected *beams* of pure white light – *illuminating* the darkest corners of the Cathedral.

"Can you see him anywhere?" Miss Elliot asked and *inspected* the *aisles* on the left side of the *nave*.
Inspector Hudson, who was *inspecting* the *aisles* on the right, answered, "No, I'm afraid not. Maybe it is best if we split up," he suggested.
"Good idea!" replied Miss Elliot. "I'll check out the Stone Gallery and you can check out the Golden Gallery."

"Golden Gallery?" the inspector asked confused.
"Yes, it's one of the external galleries which runs over there."
Miss Elvira pointed towards the outer *boundaries* of the Cathedral.
"Ah, that's what they call that area," remarked Inspector Hudson.
"Let's meet in the Whispering Gallery in fifteen minutes," Miss Elliot *carried on*.
"Okay, I know where that is. I'll see you then." The two *investigators* parted.

> *Übung 27: Setzen Sie die richtigen Pronomen ein!*
> *(him, mine (2x), his, me, your, them)*

1. Excuse _____!

2. He told _____ that they had the wrong guy.

3. To _____ disappointment he had arrested the wrong man.

4. "The turban does not belong to me, it isn't _____."

5. The inspector recognized the man. He had seen _____ before.

6. "That was _____ idea to talk to him, not _____!"

After fifteen minutes they met at the top of the Whispering Gallery which runs around the *interior* of the *dome*. It gets its name from the special construction of the *dome*. A whisper against the wall at any point is *audible* to a listener with their ear held to a point on exactly the opposite side. Whispering voices were echoing off the walls. It sounded like the ghostly echoes of long-lost souls.
"Any luck?" the inspector asked.

"I'm afraid not; and you?"
Inspector Hudson shook his head.
"So what do we do now?" Miss Elliot *inquired*.
James Hudson caught a *glimpse* of the cathedral *caretaker*, who was wearing a grey overall and *inspecting* a *pillar*.
"Let's ask that gentleman if he saw our prince," suggested the inspector.
"Why not!" remarked Miss Elliot.

Übung 28: Übersetzen Sie die Sätze im Konditional!

1. Inspector Hudson würde niemals Miss Elliot sein Auto fahren lassen.

   Inspector Hudson would never let Miss Elliot drive his car.

2. Elvira Elliot würde nie zugeben, dass sie zu schnell Auto fährt.

   _____

3. Inspector Hudson würde niemals alleine die „Flüstergalerie" finden.

   _____

4. Prince Vikram würde niemals ohne Turban aus dem Haus gehen.

   _____

5. Sir Reginald würde sehr gerne den Dieb schnappen.

   _____

6. Miss Elliot würde immer mit dem Inspektor zusammenarbeiten.

_____

The *investigators* introduced themselves to the *caretaker* and asked about the prince.

"You could not miss him," said the *caretaker*. "He walked in here with a *bunch of people*. There were about ten or fifteen of them. Their limousines were parked right outside the door – caused quite a *commotion*."

"Did you *by any chance* hear where their next destination was?"

"I could not tell you for sure, but the Indian fellow with the flashy *gem* was really *keen on* seeing Westminster Abbey."

"I see," the inspector said. "Well, thank you very much!"

"Any time!" the *caretaker* replied.

Miss Elliot and Inspector Hudson said goodbye and walked towards the entrance.

Übung 29: Was ist gemeint? Finden Sie den passenden Begriff!

1. a very large church _____

2. a long object which supports a building _____

3. Leonardo Da Vinci's epoch _____

4. the passage between benches _____

5. the holy table in a church _____

6. the central part of a church _____

7. a person who looks after a building _____

Elvira Elliot and Inspector Hudson arrived at Westminster Abbey.
"No limousines!" the inspector remarked, disappointed.
"Let's have a look anyway, you never know. Perhaps they just parked somewhere else. As you know, there are no *public parking facilities* available at the Abbey."
"Yeah, tell me about it. I used to work around the corner from here. I always took the underground Circle Line to 'Westminster' and walked."
They got out of the car. Since the car was parked illegally, Inspector Hudson leant back in and placed his police *badge* on the *dashboard*.
"That will save us from being *towed* away," the inspector said.

Übung 30: Lesen Sie weiter und setzen Sie die Verben in Klammern in die richtige Zeitform!

Just as they were walking towards the church, Inspector Hudson's mobile (1. ring) _____. He (2. answer) _____ it.

"Hello?"

"Hello, this (3. be) _____ Sir Reginald!"

"Hello, Sir!"

"How is the investigation coming along? Have you (4. find) _____ Marc Drum yet?"

"I'm afraid not, anything on your side?"

"No, nothing! My men (5. check) _____ hospitals, hotels, bus and train stations, and the airport – the man

(6. seem) _____ to have disappeared off the planet."

"Well, we're onto something. Mr Drum *appears* to have been (7. see) _____ some kind of Indian prince."

"A prince? That is strange. Why should he be (8. meet) _____ an Indian prince?"

"That's just what we (9. try) _____ to find out. When I (10. know) _____ more, I'll let you know."

"Sergeant Wood told me to tell you that Mr and Mrs Moore are coming to the station later."
"Mr and Mrs Moore?"
"Yes, you know, the couple who saw one of the thieves."
"Oh, yes of course. You must excuse my forgetfulness – too much sightseeing I guess."
"Too much what?"
"Doesn't matter! I remember they had some kind of *footage covering* the robbery. Please tell Sergeant Wood to remind them to bring their camera."
"Did nobody secure that important *evidence* last night?"
Inspector Hudson realized *straight away* that he should not have mentioned the camera to his *superior*.
"No, Sir, I'm afraid not. Don't know what went wrong," said Inspector Hudson *matter-of-factly*.
"Well, that's not very…"
Inspector Hudson interrupted Sir Reginald.
"What did you say, Sir. I think the line is going…" he *pretended*.
"I said that's not…"
"Sir, Sir? You're gone!" Inspector Hudson pressed the red button

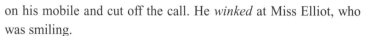

on his mobile and cut off the call. He *winked* at Miss Elliot, who was smiling.
"Was that your boss?" she asked.
"Yes, it was. These damn mobiles; they're so *unreliable* sometimes," he smiled.

Übung 31: Setzen Sie das passende Reflexivpronomen ein!

1. Miss Elliot had to force *herself* into liking Madame Tussaud's.

2. Inspector Hudson did not travel to Westminster Abbey by _____.

3. Inspector Hudson and Elvira Elliot laughed at _____.

4. Elvira Elliot asked Inspector Hudson, "Will you find the Whispering Gallery by _____?"

5. Inspector Hudson said to Sir Reginald, "We are doing all the investigating by _____."

6. Miss Elliot's car is great, but it cannot drive by _____.

Elvira Elliot and Inspector Hudson *proceeded* towards the church doors. However, when Elvira Elliot tried to open them, they did not move.
"What a *waste of time*, it's closed!" Miss Elliot exclaimed.
Inspector Hudson looked at his watch.
"It's nearly four o'clock."
Miss Elliot looked at a notice that read: "OPEN MO, TUE, THUR, FRI 09:30-15:45; WED 09:30-18:00; SAT 09:30-13:45."

"What shall we do now?" Miss Elliot sighed.

"It's probably best we drive back to the Savoy and wait until Prince Vikram gets back."

They returned to the car.

Elvira Elliot and Inspector Hudson were driving up Brompton Road – a street located in the London district called City of Westminster. The street was *renowned for* its expensive shops, such as Harrods. It started from Knightsbridge *tube* station and ran south west through an extremely wealthy *residential area*. As well as the top shops, there are also five-star hotels and many top restaurants to be found on Brompton Road.

> **! ÜBUNG 32**
>
> *Übung 32: Lesen Sie weiter und unterstreichen Sie die Übersetzungen der Substantive in Klammern!*
>
> ***(1. Bremsen 2. Reifen 3. Herzanfall 4. Leute 5. Laden 6. Blick 7. Edelstein)***

Just as the red car was shooting past Harrods, Elvira Elliot all of a sudden hit the brakes. The car's tyres *squealed* and Inspector Hudson nearly had a heart attack.

"What on earth are you doing – trying to kill us?" he said angrily.

"No, trying to help us!" was her answer.

Miss Elliot put the car into *reverse* and *approached* Harrods. Cars were *tooting* and people shouting at them. Elvira Elliot did not seem to care. She came to a halt in front of Harrods and pointed behind them. Inspector Hudson turned around and saw three big limousines parked in front of the store.

"I think I just saw Prince Vikram walk in. I caught a *glimpse* of a white turban and something *flashed* in the light. I *assume* that was his *scarlet gem*," Elvira Elliot said.

"Well, I didn't see anything. On the other hand I'm not surprised, due to the speed you were going."

Inspector Hudson and Elvira Elliot entered Harrods, an *upmarket* and exclusive department store.
"We'll need to hurry and find the prince before we lose him again. This place is enormous. I read in some women's magazine that the store has over 92,000 *square metres* of selling space."
Inspector Hudson was impressed.
"I didn't know women's magazines could be so informative," he remarked.
The *investigators* eventually found Prince Vikram in the great Food Hall, which is world-famous for the *abundance* and quality of its *merchandise*. Everything looked so fresh and inviting: the large grapefruits looked like miniature suns *beaming* red and orange. Bright red juicy tomatoes stood right next to fresh *crisp* salads. Unusual fruits, rich green vegetables and fresh herbs filled the air with exotic and appetizing *scents*.

Übung 33: Welche Wörter gehören zusammen?

1. Brompton Road
2. City of Westminster
3. tyres
4. horn
5. metre
6. Harrods
7. area
8. Savoy
9. Crown Jewels

- [ ] shop
- [ ] toot
- [ ] residential
- [ ] car
- [ ] borough
- [ ] square
- [ ] street
- [ ] Tower of London
- [ ] hotel

Elvira Elliot and Inspector Hudson *approached* Prince Vikram. Before they could get near him, however, they were surrounded by tall, muscular men in dark suits.

"What do you want?" one of them *barked*.

Inspector Hudson showed them his police *badge*.

"We'd like to talk to Prince Vikram regarding a very important matter."

"What matter?" another bodyguard asked.

"I can only talk about it to him personally."

"Well then, you don't talk to him at all."

Inspector Hudson *smirked*.

"Do you rehearse this?" he asked *mockingly*.

"Why don't you just *beat it*, *copper*?"

"I'd watch my mouth if I were you!" Inspector Hudson replied.

People were starting to stare. Some of them pointed, others whispered to each other.

> *Übung 34: Lesen Sie weiter und unterstreichen Sie im Text die Synonyme der Wörter in Klammern!*
> **(1. shining 2. speak 3. issue 4. elegantly 5. undisclosed 6. to escort)**

Suddenly the prince seemed to notice what was going on and came over to see what all the *commotion* was about. He was a very handsome man with dark sparkling eyes which even *outshone* the *scarlet gem* on his white turban.

"Now, now gentlemen," he said to his bodyguards in perfect English. "What is all the *fuss* about?"

"This policeman here says he would like to talk to you."

"Does he now," the prince remarked.

"Yes, he does!" Inspector Hudson said.

"In what matter, may I ask?"

"It has something to with the investigations into the robbery of the Kohinoor diamond," Inspector Hudson said very quietly. "My name is Inspector James Hudson from the London police and this is a colleague of mine, Miss Elvira Elliot."

The prince *bowed gracefully.*

"Well, you obviously *appear* to know who I am. I read about the robbery in the newspaper – it is a great loss, I must say."

"Maybe we can talk somewhere private," Inspector Hudson suggested.

"Yes, of course. If you would like to *accompany* me to my car – nobody will disturb us there."

Elvira Elliot and Inspector Hudson sat in the back of Prince Vikram's limousine. It had very comfortable seats and was *equipped* with a mini bar and a television in the back. Prince Vikram sat opposite them – a distance of at least two metres between them. He smiled warmly at Miss Elliot and looked deep into her eyes. Then he turned his attention towards the inspector.

"Now how can I *be of assistance*?" he asked.

"Do you know a man called Marc Drum?" Elvira Elliot asked.

"Yes, we met a couple of times – has something happened to him?" the prince *inquired*, full of concern.

"We're not quite sure about that, he has disappeared. Nobody has seen him since the robbery in the Tower of London."

"I see," said the prince, understanding immediately that Marc Drum was obviously a main *suspect*.

"So what was your relationship with this man, Prince Vikram?" Inspector Hudson asked.

"That is a simple question to answer: I'm planning to make a documentary about the 'long journey' of the Kohinoor. Over the centuries, the diamond has travelled around almost the whole world."

Übung 35: Wie heißt das Wort auf Englisch?

1. rückwärts fahren
2. endlich
3. Polizeimarke
4. geschlossen
5. unzuverlässig
6. Öffnungszeiten
7. eintreten
8. sich verbeugen
9. Verdächtiger

The prince smiled warmly at Miss Elliot. She smiled back a little *self-consciously*.

"And what did this have to do with Marc Drum?" the inspector asked in a *firm* tone, trying to put a stop to the *flirtatious* atmosphere developing between the prince and his colleague.

„I interviewed him about the '*Ceremony of the Keys*' and his work in the Tower. I was also looking for a real *Beefeater* to take on a short part in my film."

"That's all?"

"Yes, that's all there was to it."

"When was the last time you saw Mr Drum?" Elvira Elliot asked in a kind, warm voice, which was very unlike her normal style.

"I think it must have been two or three days ago. I would have to look in my diary to be sure."

"We believe you, Prince Vikram. There's no need for that," smiled Elvira Elliot.

Übung 36: Steigern Sie die folgenden Adjektive!

1. long — *longer* — *longest*
2. deep — _____ — _____
3. nice — _____ — _____
4. helpful — _____ — _____
5. narrow — _____ — _____
6. exhausted — _____ — _____
7. bad — _____ — _____
8. comfortable — _____ — _____

Inspector Hudson tried to keep his *outrage* to himself.
"Well, that will be all for now," he said.
"I was glad I could *be of assistance*."
Prince Vikram got out his card and *handed* it to Miss Elliot.
"You can call me anytime", Prince Vikram paused and looked intensely at Elvira Elliot, "if you have any further questions."
They all got out of the limousine and said goodbye. Prince Vikram returned to Harrods, the *investigators headed for* their car.

*Übung 37: Setzen Sie die Wörter **since**, **for**, **ago** in die Sätze richtig ein!*

1. Miss Elvira spotted the prince five minutes _____.
2. Prince Vikram has been staying in the Savoy _____ Monday.

3. Months _____, Inspector Hudson dealt with a similar case.

4. Marc Drum has been missing _____ two days.

5. Inspector Hudson has not been on holiday _____ August.

6. Mrs Drum has been married to Mr Drum _____ years.

7. Prince Vikram has not seen Marc Drum _____ two days.

"Well, that wasn't very professional, was it?" the inspector said, with irritation.
"Do you think so, Inspector?" Miss Elliot *mocked* him. "You're not jealous, are you?"
"Certainly not!" he exclaimed.
Inspector Hudson held out his hand, *palm* upwards. Elvira Elliot looked at him in surprise.
"What?"
"Give me the car keys!" he said *firmly*. I've had enough of your *roller-coaster* driving techniques for one day!"
Elvira Elliot *tutted* and placed the car keys into his *palm*.
"Fine!" she said, *aggravated*. "But get us to the police station before tomorrow morning, please!"

Übung 38: *Haben die Wörter dieselbe Bedeutung? Markieren Sie: richtig ✔ oder falsch – !*

1. hand/give ☐
2. Miss/Ms ☐
3. outrage/anger ☐
4. relieved/glad ☐
5. help/betray ☐
6. assistance/helper ☐

5. Smoke and Shadows

Mr and Mrs Moore were staying at a two-star hotel on Piccadilly Circus. They walked down the stairs and out onto the street.
"So what's the best way to get to Scotland Yard?" Mrs Moore asked her husband.
Mr Moore took an underground map out of his bag and studied it.

Übung 39: Lesen Sie weiter und unterstreichen Sie die englische Übersetzung der Wörter in Klammern!
(1. Verbindung 2. stolz 3. klingt 4. Haltestellen 5. zögerte 6. Indizien 7. aufklären)

"Let me see... Ah, here we are. We have to get on the Piccadilly Line here at Piccadilly Circus and get off at South Kensington, where there's a connection to the Circle Line. From there it's only two more stops to Victoria Street, where Scotland Yard is located."
"Well, that sounds simple enough," said Mrs Moore. "Did you remember the camera?"
"Of course, dear!" answered Mr Moore, *patting* his camera bag.
"Good! The police seem to think there could be very important *clues* on the *footage*. Who knows – we might help them solve the crime," said Mrs Moore proudly.
"Just as well I filmed then, eh?" Mr Moore said excitedly.

Mrs Moore hesitated and looked at her husband.
"Yes, maybe it was," she answered sceptically.
Mrs Moore looked at her watch.
"Oh, we'd better hurry along, I told Inspector Hudson we'd be there at six p.m. I don't want to keep him waiting."

Mr and Mrs Moore walked towards the underground.

Mr and Mrs Moore were standing in the underground station waiting for the train to arrive.

"I really wonder what Scotland Yard is like. I've only ever seen it on TV," Mrs Moore said.

Mr Moore got out his tourist guide of London and *flicked through* the pages.

"It says here that Scotland Yard is the *headquarters* of the Metropolitan Police Service, responsible for policing Greater London. It occupies a 20-storey office block."

"Why, that's huge, isn't it?" Mrs Moore said, impressed. "I wonder what the view is like from the top."

Übung 40: Ersetzen Sie das unterstrichene Wort durch das Gegenteil!

1. They were <u>walking</u> in the underground station. _____

2. Inspector Hudson has <u>often</u> met Prince Vikram. _____

3. Scotland Yard's office building is <u>huge</u>. _____

4. Mrs Moore was very <u>excited</u> about going to Scotland Yard. _____

5. Mr Moore <u>hates</u> filming. _____

6. The Moores walked <u>away from</u> the underground. _____

7. Scotland Yard is <u>easy</u> to find. _____

A dark figure was *making* its *way* towards the area where Mr and Mrs Moore were standing. They were so busy talking that they did not see the person *approach*. The dark figure managed to get right up to the Moores. The person *grabbed* the camera bag which Mr Moore was carrying over his shoulder.

"Hey!" Mr Moore shouted and turned around.

He nearly *jumped out of his skin* when he saw the masked person. The dark figure *tugged* at the bag. Mr Moore would not let it go.

"Get off, you *scoundrel*!" he cried.

However, the mysterious person was stronger; he pulled the bag off Mr Moore's shoulder and ran. Mr and Mrs Moore chased the thief, who was already disappearing into the crowd.

"Stop him! Stop him!" Mr Moore cried.

Übung 41: Wie lauten die Imperative auf Englisch? Übersetzen Sie!

1. Geh! _____

2. Haltet sie! _____

3. Sag ihm das nicht! _____

4. Hör auf damit! _____

5. Lass mich in Ruhe! _____

6. Bleib hier! _____

The Moores got to the underground steps that led towards ground level. They were out of breath. The thief was far ahead. There was no chance of them catching him now. Just as he was climbing the last step, something fell out of his pocket – the thief did not notice and disappeared onto Piccadilly Circus.

"I think I have seen that person before – those *piercing* dark brown eyes…Yes, it was the same person in black I saw at the Tower of London." Mr Moore *shuddered* and held on to the railing, puffing and panting.

"Well, that's the film *footage* gone!" sighed Mrs Moore, who was also breathing very heavily.

Mr Moore smiled and started to *fumble* around in his coat pocket.

"What are you smiling about? I don't think it's very funny!" Mrs Moore exclaimed.

Mr Moore took a cassette out of his pocket and waved it *slyly*.

"The cassette isn't in the camera. It's here."

Mrs Moore smiled back.

"Well done, Kevin, well done!" she *praised* him.

Mrs Moore started walking up the stairs.

"Where are you going?" Mr Moore asked.

"I'm going to get that knife the thief dropped. If that was the thief from the Tower, then that knife he dropped is *vital evidence*."

Mrs Moore *made* her *way* towards the knife lying at the top of the stairs.

! *Übung 42: Beantworten Sie die Fragen zum Text!*

1. Where were Mr and Mrs Moore staying?

_____

2. Was the underground near the hotel?

_____

3. Why do the police think Mr and Mrs Moore can help them?

_____

4. Was the thief in the underground the same thief who stole the Kohinoor diamond?

___

5. What fell out of the thief's pocket?

___

6. Did the thief manage to steal the tape?

___

7. Which underground lines did the Moores take?

___

It was 6:40 p.m. by the time Mr and Mrs Moore reached Scotland Yard. They were taken immediately to Inspector Hudson's office, where he and Miss Elliot were waiting for them impatiently. Mr and Mrs Moore told him exactly what had happened.
"And you believe it to be the same person you saw during the robbery at the Tower?"
"Yes, definitely! I'll never forget those dark brown eyes."
"What height would you say the person was?"
"I'd say around 1.75m," Mr Moore answered.
"Anything else you noticed about the person – anything *distinctive*?"
"Not really," Mrs Moore replied. "Although the person was very slim…and built more like a woman than a man."
"Interesting!" Inspector Hudson remarked. "And that's all?"
"Yes, that's all we can really say about the thief."
"Well, if it was the same person, then he was obviously trying to get the tape," the inspector said.

Übung 43: Welcher Satz enthält die richtige Zeitform? Kreuzen Sie an!

1. Mr und Mrs Moore gingen die Treppe herunter.
   a) ☐ Mr and Mrs Moore walk down the stairs.
   b) ☐ Mr and Mrs Moore walked down the stairs.
   c) ☐ Mr and Mrs Moore had walked down the stairs.

2. Sie waren außer Atem.
   a) ☐ They were out of breath.
   b) ☐ They were going out of breath.
   c) ☐ They will be going out of breath.

3. Mr and Mrs Moore spazierten gerade zur U-Bahn.
   a) ☐ Mr and Mrs Moore walked to the underground.
   b) ☐ Mr and Mrs Moore walk to the underground.
   c) ☐ Mr and Mrs Moore were walking to the underground.

4. Inspector Hudson hat schon viele Fälle gelöst.
   a) ☐ Inspector Hudson solved many cases.
   b) ☐ Inspector Hudson has solved many cases.
   c) ☐ Inspector Hudson solves many cases.

5. Früher hat Mr Moore mehr fotografiert.
   a) ☐ Mr Moore used to take more pictures.
   b) ☐ Mr Moore was taking pictures earlier than usual.
   c) ☐ Mr Moore takes pictures early.

"I wonder how he knew about the *footage* and where to find Mr and Mrs Moore?" Elvira Elliot asked. "Only Marc Drum knew that Mr Moore was filming the *commotion* at the Tower."

"Has Mr Drum still not turned up?" Mrs Moore asked. "We read in the morning newspaper that he had *vanished*."

"No, I'm afraid not. He's still missing."

"Do you think he is in on the robbery?" Mr Moore *inquired*.

"Sorry, I can't answer your question – police internal information, if you know what I mean."

"Oh, of course, I understand completely," Mr Moore said.

"Well, thank you for bringing round the film material and answering our questions. You've been very helpful; we'll *be in touch*," Inspector Hudson said.

Mr and Mrs Moore shook hands with the inspector and Miss Elliot. Just as they were walking out of the door, Mrs Moore turned around.

"Oh, I nearly forgot!" she exclaimed. "The knife!"

Mrs Moore opened her handbag and took the folding knife out. Its silver handle *sparkled* in the office light.

"A knife?" the inspector asked.

"Yes, the thief dropped it as he escaped from the train."

Mrs Moore gave it to Inspector Hudson. He took a *handkerchief* out of his pocket and *took hold of* the knife. He looked at it in amazement and opened up the *blade*. The inspector *scrutinized* it.

"Very interesting, very interesting indeed," he remarked.

"It's beautiful, isn't it?" Mrs Moore said.

"Yes, it shows great *craftsmanship*."

Inspector Hudson *handed* it in the *handkerchief* to Miss Elliot. She looked at it – turning it around in her hand.

"What do you think?" the inspector asked.

"I'm not quite sure. Knives are not my speciality; however, it wasn't cheap, that's for sure. I'll have to do some research."

"Yes, and we'll have to check it for fingerprints as well," the inspector added, still looking at the knife.

Then he looked at Mr and Mrs Moore. He was very pleased with them.

"Thanks for your cooperation! You don't happen to be looking for a job with the London police," the inspector joked.

Mr and Mrs Moore shook their heads, smiling.

"No, thank you!" they *declined*. "I think we've had enough crime action to last us a lifetime."

Mr and Mrs Moore said goodbye and left the office.

> **!** *Übung 44: Lesen Sie weiter und tragen Sie die Vergangenheitsform der angegebenen Verben ein!*

Elvira Elliot (1. pick) _____ up the knife again.

"Looks like something that could belong to an Indian prince," she remarked.

"What are you getting at?" (2. ask) _____ the inspector, *puzzled*.

"I don't know, just a theory: Dark brown eyes, around 1.75m, *narrow-shouldered* and slim, and this extraordinary knife."

"We shouldn't *jump to conclusions* now, Miss Elliot. And anyway, I (3. think) _____ he was your new best friend?"

Elvira Elliot (4. laugh) _____.

"I (5. know) _____ you were jealous, Inspector!" Elvira Elliot (6. tease) _____ him.

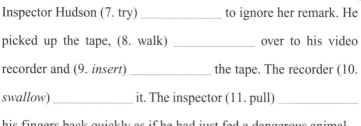

Inspector Hudson (7. try) _____ to ignore her remark. He picked up the tape, (8. walk) _____ over to his video recorder and (9. *insert*) _____ the tape. The recorder (10. *swallow*) _____ it. The inspector (11. pull) _____ his fingers back quickly as if he had just fed a dangerous animal.

"And just because I thought him to be stunningly attractive does not mean I believe he is as good a man as he looks."
"Well, you could have fooled me," the inspector *mumbled*.
"What?"
"I said: What motive do you think he has?"
"Oh, I thought that's what you said," Elvira Elliot *mocked* Inspector Hudson.
The inspector just *grunted*. He was desperately trying to find the video channel on the television.
"Are you all right there?" Elvira Elliot *inquired*.
"Yes, I'm perfectly fine!" Inspector Hudson answered, sounding irritated, while he nervously *fumbled* about with the *remote control*.
Elvira Elliot sighed.
"Anyway, as I told you this morning, India has claimed to be the *rightful* owner of the Kohinoor diamond more than once," she explained.
"Yes, I guess that could be a motive. It would also explain why only the Kohinoor was stolen and nothing else. Last but not least, he did meet up with our main *suspect,* Marc Drum. However, I'm not quite sure if we're on the right track there – after all, he is friendly with the Royal Family."
"Maybe you're right. Let's put Prince Vikram to one side for now and see what the video has to offer."

Übung 45: Welches Wort ist das „schwarze Schaf"?

1. suspect, disregard, guess, assume
2. last, second, first, three
3. motive, aim, why, reason
4. worse, worst, terrible, bad
5. perfectly, carefully, sadly, good
6. day, morning, afternoon, evening
7. track, search, hunt, path

Inspector Hudson started the tape. At first, all they could see and hear was smoke and people shouting and screaming. The camera work was also very shaky.

"That looks *terrifying*," Miss Elliot commented on the *footage*.

"It sure does!" the inspector said.

He *fast-forwarded* the tape until he got to the bit where they could hear the *Beefeater* shouting for help. They could hear his voice, but he could not be seen. There was still a lot of smoke around and the camera was constantly shaking. You could also hear Mr and Mrs Moore's voices commenting on what was happening. They *made* their *way* towards the *Beefeater*. The smoke had cleared a little and Inspector Hudson and Elvira Elliot saw Marc Drum sitting against the wall. He was holding his *bleeding* head.

"It certainly looks like a real wound to me," Elvira Elliot said. Suddenly Mr Moore moved the camera down.

"What is he doing!" exclaimed Miss Elliot. "It was just starting to get interesting!"

"He's probably trying to help Marc Drum to his feet," answered the inspector. "But I think I'll *rewind* it back to the bit where he was *approaching* Marc Drum and put the *recording* into slow motion – maybe we missed something."

"I was looking very carefully. I don't think there was anything to see," Miss Elliot said.
"Just wait and see. This is the latest technology. I can even zoom in on things like that."

Übung 46: Welche Gegenteile gehören zusammen? Ordnen Sie zu!

1. real
2. hold
3. fast-forward
4. miss
5. clear
6. whisper
7. record

- [ ] let go
- [ ] play
- [ ] hit
- [ ] vague
- [ ] rewind
- [ ] false
- [ ] scream

Miss Elvira folded her arms and watched the inspector sceptically. Inspector Hudson *rewound* the tape. He pressed the play button, but the tape kept on *rewinding*.
"Oh, this is such a stupid thing!" he complained.
Elvira Elliot rolled her eyes, but said nothing.
Inspector Hudson eventually managed to get the *recording* to where he wanted it and played the whole scene again in slow motion.
"All I can see is slow smoke!" *mocked* Miss Elliot.
Inspector Hudson ignored her. He was concentrating on what was happening on the screen. Suddenly, just faintly through the smoke, two shadows were visible.
"What's that?" Miss Elliot exclaimed.
One of the dark figures *appeared* to be a *Beefeater*. You could tell by the shape of the hat. He seemed to be gesturing.

> *Übung 47: Lesen Sie weiter und unterstreichen Sie alle sechs Adverbien im folgenden Abschnitt!*

Inspector Hudson turned around and smiled triumphantly.

"Looks like our *Beefeater* had a lively conversation before he was hit on the head."

The *recording* went on. They could see the *Beefeater handing* something to the person dressed in black.

"Was that the *Queen's Keys*?" Elvira Elliot asked.

She moved up closer to the screen so she could see exactly what was going on.

"I'm quite sure it was the *Queen's Keys*," the inspector answered calmly.

With amazement, Elvira Elliot and Inspector Hudson watched the person in black hitting Marc Drum hard on the head. He fell to the ground. The black figure disappeared as if it had become *invisible*.

"Where did he go?" Miss Elliot exclaimed.

"No, idea!" *shrugged* the inspector. "But it might be the same person Mr Moore ran into earlier. Remember he said he was a fast mover – like an animal of prey."

"Wow!" said Elvira Elliot. "It's like in one of these crime movies!"

Inspector Hudson shook his head *disapprovingly*.

"Nothing we experience on a day-to-day basis has anything to do with crime movies!" he said, almost *reproachfully*.

Elvira Elliot *shrugged*.

"If you say so – I didn't know you *detested* crime fiction."

"I don't *detest* it; I just don't think it's very realistic. But let's turn our attention back to the *recording*. It certainly looks like Marc Drum is in on the robbery."

"Yes, there's no doubt about that. His whole *alleged* injury was a

set-up and he obviously *deliberately deceived* the other guards."
"That's right. And now we know for sure why he went missing – or perhaps I should say why he has *gone into hiding*."
"So that's one down, but who are his *accomplices*?"
"Good question. At least we know for sure that Marc Drum has something to do with the robbery; and he could never have *pulled it off* on his own."
"Yes, and one of his *accomplices* seems to have some kind of artistic skills. We're looking for someone who does gymnastics, climbing or specializes in some form of *martial arts*."
"And who obviously has a taste for extravagant knives," Miss Elliot added, pointing to the knife lying on the table.
Inspector Hudson nodded, agreeing fully with Miss Elliot.

*Übung 48: Setzen Sie die richtige Zukunftsform **will** oder **going to** in die Lücken ein!*

1. "Don't worry, we _____ find the thieves soon!" Inspector Hudson said to Sir Reginald.

2. Miss Elliot and the inspector _____ have the knife examined.

3. Inspector Hudson _____ catch the thieves if it is the last thing he ever does.

4. Mrs Moore says she _____ help find the thief.

5. The investigators _____ look for an acrobat.

6. I have decided that I _____ become a policeman.

"Let's have another look at the tape," suggested the inspector. "Maybe I can identify somebody in the crowd – a known criminal for example. It wouldn't surprise me if the robbers had somebody in amongst the tourists."

"Well, maybe you're right," sighed Miss Elliot. "I just hope my eyes aren't square by the end of the night."

Inspector Hudson *rewound* the tape and replayed it again.

Übung 49: Bilden Sie die Verlaufsform mit *we are*!

1. take
2. prefer
3. travel
4. lie
5. run
6. hum

Two hours later they were still analysing the tape. However, they did not see anything suspicious.

"Oh, not again!" Miss Elliot exclaimed as Inspector Hudson *rewound* the tape once more. "We've already watched it about ten times."

"Just once more and then we can finish for the night."

"If you must!" answered Elvira Elliot, a little annoyed.

The inspector was watching the tape *recording* again. Elvira Elliot was falling asleep. All of a sudden he let out a cry: "I've got something. At last! I knew there was something out there!"

Elvira Elliot *started* out of her *slumber* and moved up to the screen.

Übung 50: Lesen Sie weiter und setzen Sie für die Wörter in Klammern deren Gegenteil ein!

Inspector Hudson pointed at a middle-aged (1. hairy) _____ man with a *moustache*. He was in amongst a crowd of people rushing (2. away from) _____ the Tower exit.

"That's David Bucket!" he exclaimed.

"Who is David Bucket?" Miss Elliot (3. replied) _____.

"He's a known criminal – has done a few bank robberies in his time. He just got out of jail not too (4. short) _____ ago. I wonder what he is doing there."

"He's probably not there to enjoy the *Ceremony of the Keys*," Elvira Elliot remarked dryly.

"You can be (5. uncertain) _____ about that. I think we should pay him a visit. I'll get one of my men to find out where he is (6. dying) _____ and then we'll bring him in."

"If he has not disappeared like Marc Drum has," Miss Elliot said.

"Let's (7. to fear) _____ not." Inspector Hudson looked at his watch. "It's (8. early) _____. We should get some sleep."

Elvira Elliot stretched and *yawned*. "Yes, (9. bad) _____ idea. It's been a very long day."

"It sure has been. My men will see to David Bucket. If they get him tonight, we can question him first thing in the morning."
The inspector and Miss Elliot left the office.

6. Mingling with the Stars

The next day, Elvira Elliot and Inspector Hudson were sitting in the inspector's office at Scotland Yard again. The inspector was sitting in his chair and Miss Elliot was leaning against the wall. They were both drinking a steaming cup of tea when the office door opened. Sir Reginald walked in *briskly*. He was carrying newspapers under his arm.
"Good morning, Miss Elliot, good morning, Inspector!"
"Good morning!" they answered.
"What was all this about?"
Sir Reginald put the morning newspaper on the table. There was a huge picture of the inspector, showing him pushing a camera man away. It looked very violent. The *headline* was: "London Police Take Brutal Measures!" Inspector Hudson looked at the paper. He *shrugged* and took a sip of tea.
"I was just getting them off Mrs Drum's *premises* – they had no right to be there," the inspector said calmly.
"Well, it was also wrong of you to push them onto the street so violently," Sir Reginald said, a little angrily.
Inspector Hudson looked over at Elvira Elliot, who smiled *reassuringly* at him.
"They just wouldn't leave poor Mrs Drum alone," she *intervened*. "What Inspector Hudson did was fully justified."
Sir Reginald looked back and forth between the inspector and Miss Elliot. Despite his anger he had to smile.

"You two seem to be getting along fine these days," he said, with a slight hint of sarcasm in his voice.

Sir Reginald opened up another newspaper. The *headline* read: "Scotland Yard still fishing in the dark. Has the Kohinoor diamond gone forever?" He showed them another *headline*: "What's next – Buckingham Palace?"

Übung 51: Lesen Sie weiter und unterstreichen Sie das im Kontext passende Wort!

"As you can see, the (1.) *pressure*/television is on. You know I hate bad (2.) people/publicity and as you can imagine, my phone has not stopped (3.) ringing/knocking all morning: The *Home Secretary*, the Queen's private (4.) secretary/guard – to name but two! So tell me, Inspector, how is the (5.) invasion/investigation coming along?"

"I'm glad you *got round to* that, Sir," the inspector said, (6.) relieved/released.

"First of all, we have (7.) *evidence*/confirmation that Marc Drum has something to do with the robbery."

"Marc Drum – the Chief *Yeoman Warder*?" Sir Reginald asked in (8.) disbelieve/disbelief.

"Yes, I'm afraid so!"

"Oh dear, of all things…" Sir Reginald was lost for words. "This country is going downhill faster than I thought! No room for honour and integrity anymore, eh?" he *carried on* in a very disappointed, almost sad tone. "Why would he do such a thing – a man of his position?"

"We don't know yet. He might have money problems we *are*

unaware of; he might have been forced into doing it. At the moment we have no answers to that question," answered Inspector Hudson.

"Do you have any answers at all?" asked Sir Reginald impatiently. The Inspector took a deep breath. He was trying to control his anger.

"Yes, in fact we do! We know Drum had probably at least two *accomplices*. We have already identified one of the *suspects*. His name is David Bucket. My men have found out that he works as a *caretaker* at Madame Tussaud's. We're going to take him in for questioning as soon as he shows up at work."

"And the second *accomplice*?"

"We don't know the identity of the second person. However, we have a vague description of him. We also believe him to be an expert in gymnastics or acrobatics."

"I see," Sir Reginald said thoughtfully.

At that moment someone knocked on the door. Sergeant Wood entered. He greeted everyone and turned his attention towards the inspector.

"I've just been contacted by our man observing Madame Tussaud's. David Bucket has arrived."

"Very good, Sergeant!" Inspector Hudson said and *grabbed* his coat. "Let's go and arrest him!"

Elvira Elliot, Sergeant Wood and the inspector said goodbye to Sir Reginald. He wished them luck.

ÜBUNG 52

*Übung 52: Vervollständigen Sie die Sätze mit **ago**, **during**, oder **last**!*

1. Sir Reginald walked into Inspector Hudson's office _____ his tea break.

2. _____ week's newspaper was full of bad news.

3. It was a while _____ since Reginald had been so angry.

4. Elvira Elliot lost her purse _____ Wednesday.

5. He was much happier two weeks _____.

6. The suspect was very nervous _____ the interview.

Inspector Hudson, Elvira Elliot, Sergeant Wood and three uniformed policemen stood on the pavement at the opposite side of the road from Madame Tussaud's – a very famous wax figure museum in London. It was originally founded by the wax *sculptress* Marie Tussaud in 1835. At that time, the wax museum had been located in Baker Street. Today, Madam Tussaud's is located on Marylebone Road in London. Walking along the street one can hardly miss the museum because of its *distinctive* green *dome*-shaped roof.

Übung 53: Setzen Sie, wenn nötig, das passende Relativpronomen ein!

1. Inspector Hudson, _____ works for Scotland Yard, told his men exactly what to do.

2. David Bucket works at Madame Tussaud's, _____ is on Marylebone Road.

3. The investigators don't know _____ the second thief is.

4. The day _____ the robbery occurred, David Bucket was at the Tower.

5. Marie Tussaud was the woman _____ founded Madame Tussaud's.

6. Elvira Elliot, _____ hair is red, likes the Savoy.

"When does the museum open?" Inspector Hudson asked Sergeant Wood.
"It opens at 9:30 a.m."
The inspector looked at his watch.
"That means we have half an hour to bring David Bucket in, before the museum opens. We don't want to cause any publicity whatsoever. And we should create as little of a *fuss* as possible," Inspector Hudson instructed his men. They nodded approvingly. With this, the policemen and Miss Elliot started to walk across the road, *heading* straight towards the entrance of Madame Tussaud's.
The woman behind the ticket counter did not even look up when Inspector Hudson stood in front of her.
"We don't open until half past nine!" she said.

Übung 54: Schreiben Sie die Uhrzeit aus!

1. 06:30   *half past six*
2. 10:10   _____
3. 03:15   _____
4. 08:35   _____
5. 12:45   _____
6. 07:55   _____
7. 05:05   _____

Inspector Hudson placed his *badge* on the counter. The woman looked up. She *started* when she saw the large group of policemen standing in front of her. She looked nervously at Inspector Hudson and then at his *badge*.

"Is there anything wrong?" she asked, looking up *anxiously* again.

"Nothing to be alarmed about," the inspector answered. "Where can we find Mr David Bucket?"

"David?" she asked in *astonishment*. "He should be doing his rounds, checking the wax figures – seeing if everything is in place. If you just walk in that direction, you will find him."

Inspector Hudson thanked the woman. He and his men *headed for* the wax figure show rooms. They walked past celebrities, politicians, well-known actors and musicians, and famous cooks such as Jamie Oliver.

Elvira Elliot looked around in amazement.

"They look so real!" she said to Inspector Hudson, looking at a wax figure of Johnny Depp. He was dressed up as a pirate.

Übung 55: Unterstreichen und verbessern Sie im folgenden Textabschnitt die sechs falsch geschriebenen Wörter!

"You can say that again!" remarcked Sergeant Wood, who was eyeing up a life-like image of Britney Spears in a very short skirt.

"Keep your eyes out for David Bucket!" the inspector *admonished* his collegue.

Inspector Hudson suddenly stoped his men. He put his finger to his lips signalling everybody to be quite. In the distance they could here somebody *whistling*. It was the tune of the song "New York, New York" by Frank Sinatra.

"That could be our man," Inspector Hudson wispered.

1. _____   4. _____

2. _____   5. _____

3. _____   6. _____

"Or it's old Frankie boy come to life!" *smirked* one of the policemen quietly.

One of his colleagues in uniform laughed as well. Inspector Hudson gave them a *disapproving* look.

They fell silent *straight away*.

"No time for jokes just now, men," he whispered. "Let's move in on Bucket, but carefully."

Elvira Elliot and the group of policemen *sneaked up* on the person, following the sound of the *whistling*. Eventually they could see a man in the distance. He was *inspecting* the wax figures.

"That's David Bucket," said the inspector in a low voice. They all tried to hide behind wax figures so that the *suspect* could not see them.

Inspector Hudson was hiding behind Winston Churchill. Elvira Elliot chose the Dalai Lama, who was smiling peacefully at *nothing in particular*.

David Bucket was standing in front of a wax figure of the Queen. He smiled at it.

"Care to dance?" he said to the Queen and *bowed*.

The policemen looked at each other. They were very amused.

"Not in the mood for talking today, eh?" David Bucket *carried on*.

"Are you sad about the Kohinoor diamond?"

David Bucket *bent* over to the Queen's ear.

"Don't worry, I'm sure it's in a safe place," he whispered and walked on, *whistling* the Frank Sinatra tune.

Übung 56: Ergänzen Sie die Sätze mit dem passenden Question Tag!

1. Inspector Hudson would never buy a sports car, *would he*?
2. Elvira Elliot would always help Inspector Hudson, _____?
3. Madame Tussaud was a very hard-working lady, _____?
4. The Dalai Lama is a very peaceful man, _____?
5. Britney Spears has great legs, _____?
6. Johnny Depp can really act, _____?
7. David Bucket stole the diamond, _____?
8. They will catch the suspect, _____?

The policemen and Elvira Elliot came out from their *hiding places* and moved on. David Bucket stopped at the Robbie Williams wax figure. He was holding two women in his arms. They were both kissing him on the cheek.

"Well, *it's all right for some*!" said David Bucket to the *motionless* figure.

Übung 57: Setzen Sie die folgenden Wörter in die Lücken!
(dashing, heading, sneak, bumped, opposite, crashed, near)

Inspector Hudson signalled to his men that it was time to arrest David Bucket. He indicated to the three uniformed policemen to (1.) _____ over to the (2.) _____ side, so that

David Bucket was surrounded by them. All of a sudden one of them accidentally knocked over one of the Spice Girls. The figure (3.) _____ to the ground. David Bucket looked up and saw the policemen. He started to run. The policemen ran after him. "Stop! Police!" they shouted.

Sergeant Wood, Elvira Elliot and Inspector Hudson followed them. They were all running through Madame Tussaud's – *dodging* famous people, (4.) _____ around stunning celebrities. Sergeant Wood (5.) _____ right into Prince Charles, he fell over. He stopped and lifted him up.

"Sorry about that!" he said as he quickly *brushed* the dust *off* of the wax figure's dinner jacket.

The sergeant ran on. (6.) _____ the entrance they were eventually catching up with David Bucket, who ran out onto the street. The policemen and Elvira Elliot were close behind him. He was running down Marylebone Street. He *appeared* to be (7.) _____ for the underground station closest to Madame Tussaud's – Baker Street.

"We need to reach him before he gets into the underground!" Inspector Hudson shouted.
He was extremely out of breath. Sergeant Wood and the three uni-

formed policemen *speeded* up. The sergeant was only two metres away from David Bucket now. He jumped and *grabbed* the *suspect's* jumper. They both fell to the ground. David Bucket tried to fight Sergeant Wood off. The three other men hurried to his assistance. *In no time* David Bucket was in handcuffs and pulled back up on his feet. Inspector Hudson and Elvira Elliot arrived.

"What do you want? I didn't do anything!" *barked* David Bucket.

"Really?" Inspector Hudson said *sardonically*. "How about stealing the Kohinoor diamond? Is that nothing?"

"That's not true!" panicked David Bucket.

"Well, we'll take you in for questioning anyway, Mr Bucket."

Two policemen took David Bucket to the police car and sat him in the backseat.

Übung 58: Setzen Sie die passende Verbform ein!

David Bucket was (1. sit) _____ in the *interrogation* room. Elvira Elliot and Inspector Hudson could (2. see) _____ him from the other side. They were behind a glass mirror.

"Do you think he'll talk?" Elvira Elliot (3. ask) _____.

"I think so – eventually," Inspector Hudson answered. "But Sergeant Wood will probably have to bluff."

Sergeant Wood (4. enter) _____ the *interrogation* room.

"So are you (5. go) _____ to tell me what exactly you were doing at the *Ceremony of the Keys*?" he asked the *suspect*.

"As I said, I wanted to see the show."

"You're still trying to tell me you were there for fun? Come on, Bucket!" the sergeant (6. exclaim) _____. "Do you really think I (7. believe) _____ you've turned into a culture lover overnight?"

"Why not?"

"Because you don't even know where Buckingham Palace is!"

"Yes, I do!" (8. insist) _____ David Bucket.

"Where is it then?"
David Bucket thought hard for a moment.
"I can't remember at the moment," he *stammered*. "But if you let me think for a minute…"
Sergeant Wood banged his fist angrily on the table.
"We don't have time for thinking!" he said impatiently. "We want the truth."
David Bucket looked upset.

! *Übung 59: Welche Substantive werden immer groß geschrieben? Kreuzen Sie an!*

1. thursday ☐
2. world war II ☐
3. prince ☐
4. doctor ☐
5. tower bridge ☐
6. december ☐
7. inspector ☐

"I'm not saying anything without my lawyer!" he exclaimed nervously.

"Lawyer?" laughed Sergeant Wood. "How are you going to explain to your lawyer that we actually have *footage* showing you holding the Kohinoor diamond?"

"What?" David Bucket asked *anxiously*.

"You heard what I said."

David Bucket looked tensely at his hands. He turned and faced the mirror. Then he looked back at the sergeant.

"You've really got me then," he said sadly.

"You can say that again, Bucket!"

David Bucket sat in silence.

"I want names. Who is in on this? Marc Drum? And who is the masked person?"

"I don't know!" *mumbled* David Bucket.

"What? Speak up, I can't hear you!"

"I said, I don't know!"

"What do you mean, you don't know?"

"I don't know if Marc Drum has anything to do with the robbery and I don't know who the masked person is."

"Well, you're a great help, aren't you?" the sergeant *mocked*. "Are you trying to tell me you're in on the robbery alone?"

"No, no – certainly not!" panicked David Bucket. "I had almost nothing to do with the whole thing!"

"You could have fooled me!"

"No, it's true. All I did was smuggle the diamond out of the Tower. The masked person gave it to me. But I have no idea who he is."

"Liar!"

"No, honest," David Bucket *stammered*. "That's all I did. All contact was done over the phone."

"What was the person's voice like?"

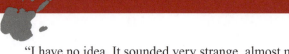

"I have no idea. It sounded very strange, almost mechanical."
"He probably used a *voice modifier*," Inspector Hudson said to Elvira Elliot. She nodded.

> **!** *Übung 60: Geben Sie die richtigen Formen von **to do** mit **he** an!*

1. einfache Gegenwart
2. Verlaufsform der Gegenwart
3. Einfache Vergangenheit
4. Verlaufsform der Vergangenheit
5. Perfekt
6. Verlaufsform des Perfekt
7. Zukunft mit "going to"
8. Zukunft mit "will"

"So what did you do with the diamond? Did you take it home and hide it in your *closet*?"
"No, I hid it in a hole beside the altar in St. Paul's Cathedral."
Elvira Elliot and Inspector Hudson looked at each other.
"I hope you are not lying again?" Sergeant Wood asked *firmly*.
"It's true. There was a loose stone, I picked it up and underneath there was a hole. I put the diamond into it."
"How much did you get for your services, Bucket?"
"Enough!"
"How much, I asked?"
"10,000 pounds!"
Sergeant Wood *whistled*.

Übung 61: Setzen Sie, wenn notwendig, den passenden Artikel ein!

1. David Bucket hid the diamond in the hole beside _____ altar.

2. For his help he did not get _____ 1,000 pounds, but actually 10,000 pounds.

3. With the money he was going to buy himself _____ new house.

4. However, David Bucket felt so bad he went to _____ church.

5. After Sergeant Wood got _____ information, he whistled.

6. It took him over two hours to get _____ truth out of him.

7. The Kohinoor diamond is kept in _____ safe place.

8. David Bucket is certainly going to _____ prison.

"Now that's a lot of money!"
"Yes, it is. I really needed it…I know it was stupid," said David Bucket in a *remorseful* voice.
"Yes, it certainly was stupid. You can say that again."
Sergeant Wood left the room. On the other side of the mirror, Inspector Hudson's mobile phone rang. It was Inspector Reid from the Murder Investigation Team.
"I thought it might interest you to know that we've just fished a body out of the Thames," Inspector Reid said dryly.
"Who?"
"We're not quite sure, but he is wearing a *Beefeater's* outfit and I somehow don't think it's a *drunk* from last year's Halloween," she answered.
"Where exactly are you?" the inspector asked.
"Very close to the Tower Bridge. You can't miss us."

"Okay, I'll be over *straight away*!"
The inspector put his mobile back in his pocket.

Übung 62: Geben Sie die Pluralform an!

1. body _____
2. river _____
3. wife _____
4. bus _____
5. sheep _____
6. day _____
7. woman driver _____
8. knife _____
9. box _____
10. policeman _____

"Who was that?"
"Inspector Reid from the Murder Investigation Team."
"Oh, that can't be good news," Miss Elliot said worriedly.
"No, it isn't. They have just fished a dead man dressed in *Beefeater* clothes out of the Thames."
"Marc Drum?" Elvira Elliot asked *anxiously*.
"They don't know yet, but we should get down there *straight away* to clarify who it is."
They opened the door and nearly *bumped into* Sergeant Wood, who was holding a cup of coffee.

Übung 63: Setzen Sie das richtige Fragewort ein!

1. _____ is Inspector Reid at the moment?

2. _____ does she work for?

3. _____ body did she find?
4. _____ part of London is she in?
5. _____ did she call Inspector Hudson?
6. _____ is her job?
7. _____ did they fish out of the Thames?
8. _____ did David Bucket hide the diamond?

"Where are you off to in such a rush? Don't you think I did a great job?"
"Excellent!" smiled Elvira Elliot.
"But I thought we could talk about it," the sergeant insisted.
"Later, Sergeant, later!" said Inspector Hudson. "We're off to the Thames."
"The Thames?" he asked, a little *puzzled*.
"Yes, they just found a body."
"Oh! I see. Anybody we know?" the sergeant asked.
"Maybe, but we'll soon see."
Elvira Elliot and Inspector Hudson said goodbye.
"What shall I do with David Bucket?" Sergeant Wood shouted to his *superior*.
"Get him a lawyer. I'm more than sure he's going to need one!" Inspector Hudson answered.

7. The Royal Suspect

Elvira Elliot and Inspector Hudson arrived at the crime scene on the banks of the River Thames near the Tower Bridge. Police lights were *flashing*, policemen and women were moving about. The two *investigators* had to fight their way through a group of *spectators* who were curious to see what was going on. The Tower Bridge was about 200 metres away from the place where the drowned *Beefeater* had been found. It was very close to the Tower of London. That's where it got its name.

! *Übung 64: Verbinden Sie die beiden Sätze, indem Sie einen zu einem Relativsatz umformulieren!*

ÜBUNG 64

1. Inspector Hudson arrived at the crime scene. It was near the Thames.

   Inspector Hudson arrived at the crime scene which was near the Thames.

2. They fought their way through curious spectators. They were in the way.

   _____

3. The Tower was close to the bridge. The Tower could be seen in the distance.

   _____

4. It was not good news. The body was found near the Thames.

   _____

5. Inspector Reid was working in the distance. She could see them coming.

   _____

6. Sergeant Wood was holding a cup of coffee. They nearly bumped into him.

The Tower Bridge, with its two tall towers, has become a well-known symbol of London. It is often wrongly called London Bridge, which is in fact the next bridge upstream.

Inspector Hudson lifted the police barrier and let Miss Elliot pass through. He followed. In the background you could see policemen dressed in white overalls; some of them were scanning the area around the body for *clues*, others were examining the body.

Inspector Reid – a tall, short-haired woman – looked up and saw Inspector Hudson. She walked towards him. They greeted each other and the inspector introduced Elvira Elliot to her.

"So what have we got?" the inspector asked, as they walked towards the body.

"The body is male, between fifty and sixty. He was obviously a *Beefeater* – he is still wearing his costume. And he probably drowned, but we won't know for sure until the autopsy has been done."

Inspector Hudson looked at Miss Elliot.

"Sounds like the man we're looking for!" he said. "Does he have a wound at the head?"

"Let's take a look."

They had almost reached the body, which was *spread* out on the bank. Inspector Reid turned to Elvira Elliot.

"It's not a pleasant sight."

"It's okay," the insurance *investigator* answered bravely. "It's not my first!"

"Oh, I see," Inspector Reid said. "But be prepared," she added.

Übung 65: *Lesen Sie weiter und unterstreichen Sie alle sieben Phrasal Verbs!*

When they reached the body, Elvira Elliot nervously *stroked* her hair away from her face. Inspector Hudson looked at her *reassuringly*. She smiled back at him.

"This is him," Inspector Reid said.

Inspector Hudson looked down at the body.

"Yes, that's Marc Drum," he said without *flinching*.

"He's been in the water for a while, that's why he's a bit *swollen* up," Inspector Reid said.

Elvira Elliot looked away.

"Are you okay?" Inspector Hudson asked. "You look a little pale."

"I'm fine," Elvira Elliot replied, pulling herself together again.

"Was he murdered?" Inspector Hudson asked Mrs Reid.

"Yes, it looks very much like it. His hands and legs were tied together. He was also weighed down by a few heavy stones."

"So do you think he was drowned somewhere near here?" the inspector asked.

"Yes, he could not get far with those weights holding him down."

Inspector Hudson looked in the direction of the Tower Bridge.

"How long do you think he has been dead?" he asked thoughtfully.

"I'd say around two, maybe three days," Inspector Reid answered.

"He could have been killed the same night as the robbery," Miss Elliot said.

"That was just what I was thinking," the inspector replied.

He turned towards Inspector Reid.

"I think we've seen enough for just now, we'll leave you to it," Inspector Hudson said to her.

Inspector Reid nodded.

"I'll keep you up to date on anything else we find out. I guess we'll know more after the autopsy."

Inspector Reid said goodbye and turned her attention back to her work. Elvira Elliot and Inspector Hudson walked away from the body.

Übung 66: Lesen Sie weiter und setzen Sie die richtige Präposition ein!

"Do you think he was murdered (1.) _____ his *accomplice*?" Miss Elliot asked.

"Could well be!"

"But why?"

"I don't know yet. But it sure doesn't look like he was murdered (2.) _____ sudden rage or something like that."

"Yes, it looks planned. Just look (3.) _____ the ropes and the heavy stones – looks very much like the murderer was prepared," Miss Elliot added.

"Maybe Marc Drum was used (4.) _____ the beginning. He was the best person to have (5.) _____ the team if you wanted to get to the Crown Jewels. He knew all the *safety regulations*, just everything."

"They must have offered him a great *reward* (6.) _____ his help. Otherwise I cannot understand why he did it."

"Yes, it is strange because only the most loyal get a job like he had," the inspector said thoughtfully. "I really do wonder what made him do it. He obviously met his murderer soon (7.) _____ the robbery – their meeting point was probably somewhere very close (8.) _____ the Tower."

"Where do we go from here?" Elvira Elliot asked.
"I guess first of all we have to tell Mrs Drum."
"Oh, dear! The poor woman will be *devastated*!" Elvira Elliot sighed.
Inspector Hudson nodded. They walked towards the car in silence.

The inspector was just about to ring Mrs Drum's doorbell when the door opened. A tall man in his mid thirties nearly *bumped into* him.
"Oh, I'm sorry!" he exclaimed.
Mrs Drum *popped* her head out.
"Inspector Hudson!" she said, sounding surprised.
"Yes, hello!" he said *grimly*.
Inspector Hudson looked at the man.
"Don't I know you from somewhere?"
The man stretched out his hand.
"Yes, Inspector, I work at the Tower. I'm a guard. We met the night of the robbery."
"Ah, yes, exactly!"
The two men shook hands.
"Mr Gunn, wasn't it?" the inspector *inquired*.
"Yes, that's me! How are things getting along, Edith and I are worried sick. Have you heard anything about Marc? You don't really believe he has anything to do with the robbery, do you?" Craig

Gunn was smiling politely at the inspector.

"My colleague and I would like to talk to Mrs Drum privately, if you don't mind," Inspector Hudson said.

"Oh, yes, of course!" Craig Gunn replied, a little *taken aback*.

He *glanced* at Edith Drum. She nodded as if to say it was okay. Craig Gunn said goodbye and left.

Übung 67: Übersetzen Sie und enträtseln Sie das Lösungswort!

1. nervös
2. Mörder
3. Kollegen
4. Zuschauer
5. zögern
6. Komplize
7. strecken

Lösung: _ _ _ _ _ _ _

"Come in!" Mrs Drum said to the *investigators*.
Elvira Elliot and Inspector Hudson entered the house.
"Are you and Mr Gunn close?" the inspector asked.
"We get along very well, yes, if that's what you mean," Mrs Drum answered. "He and my husband are good friends."
"Are they? You never mentioned that," Inspector Hudson said.
"Well, you never asked," Mrs Drum replied.
Mrs Drum led them into the living room.
"Please sit down," she said.
Elvira Elliot and Inspector Hudson did not move. They looked sad and serious. The inspector did not like the task before him.

"It's about your husband," he began carefully.

"Marc? Have you heard anything? Is he okay?"

"I'm very sorry to tell you this…but your husband is dead," Inspector Hudson said.

Edith Drum looked at the *investigators* as if she was checking to see whether this was all a big joke.

"You're serious!"

Elvira Elliot and Inspector Hudson nodded sadly. Mrs Drum put her hand to her mouth.

"Oh, my God! Oh, my God!" she kept on repeating.

! *Übung 68: Welche Sätze sind fehlerfrei? Markieren Sie mit richtig ✔ oder falsch – !*

ÜBUNG 68

1. Mrs Drum popped her head away.
2. It was the brutalest murder the inspector had ever seen.
3. Yesterday the investigators will visit Mrs Drum.
4. Tomorrow Inspector Reid is going to take a break.
5. Mrs Drum wants the thief to go to prison.
6. "You have found him, hasn't you?" Mrs Drum asked.
7. Marc Drum had been missing since three days.

Mrs Drum fell to the floor and started to *cry* her *heart out*. Miss Elliot tried to help her to her feet, but she refused to move. Edith Drum started to scream and beat her fists against the floor.

"Maybe you should call an ambulance," Miss Elliot said to the inspector. "I think she'll *crack up* if she doesn't get any *tranquilizers*."

Inspector Hudson took out his mobile phone and called an ambulance. Elvira Elliot tried to calm Mrs Drum down, but nothing helped. It did not take long for the ambulance to arrive. By this time, Edith Drum was lying *motionless* on the floor. She *appeared* to have *fainted*. The *paramedics* rushed in and took her into the ambulance. Elvira Elliot and Inspector Hudson watched it *speed* away.

Übung 69: Present Simple oder Present Progressive? Unterstreichen Sie die richtige Variante!

1. Inspector Hudson is calling/calls an ambulance at the moment.
2. Miss Elvira always drives/is driving too fast.
3. Elvira Elliot believes/is believing Mrs Drum is going to crack up.
4. Mrs Drum has/is having a nervous breakdown.
5. Calming her down does not help/is not helping.
6. Craig Gunn says/is saying goodbye and leaves/is leaving.

"Poor soul, she must have loved her husband very much!" Miss Elvira said sadly.
"Yes," Inspector Hudson sighed. "We'll have to talk to her about her husband later, when she's feeling a little better."
"I guess it's time for another tourist tour!" Miss Elliot said in a more cheerful tone.
Inspector Hudson gave her a *puzzled* look. Then all of a sudden he understood what she meant.
"Of course, St. Paul's Cathedral!" the inspector exclaimed. "Where David Bucket *allegedly* placed the Kohinoor."
"Exactly!"
"I'm already *eager* to see if his story is true."
They walked towards the car.

A little later, Elvira Elliot and Inspector Hudson entered the cathedral. As it was close to closing time, it was not as busy as on their last visit. This made the cathedral seem even larger – like the inside of some gigantic ship. The *investigators* walked up the *nave* straight towards the altar. They climbed up the stone steps and started walking around the altar.

Übung 70: Welche Synonyme gehören zusammen?

1. cathedral
2. ship
3. large
4. enter
5. understand
6. investigation
7. inside

☐ within
☐ huge
☐ comprehend
☐ boat
☐ go into
☐ enquiry
☐ church

"David Bucket said there was a loose stone here somewhere, right?" Miss Elliot asked.

"That's what he told us, anyway," the inspector said, *whilst* testing the stone floor with his foot.

"Hey, you two! What are you doing up there?" someone suddenly shouted – his voice echoing off the cold, white walls.

Inspector Hudson and Elvira Elliot looked up. A man was hurrying towards them. It was the *caretaker*; they recognized him from the last visit.

"What are you up to?" he asked them suspiciously.

Inspector Hudson showed him his police *badge*.

"Remember us? We were here yesterday. You told us about the Indian prince and his *companions*."

"Ah, yes, I remember now," the *caretaker* said, calming down. "But what in heaven's name are you looking for at the altar?"
"We are looking for a loose stone with a hole underneath," Miss Elliot answered.
"A loose stone?" the *caretaker* asked, astonished.
"Yes! Ah, here we are!" The inspector exclaimed. He *bent down* and removed a loose stone.

Übung 71: Wandeln Sie die Sätze ins Present Perfect um!

1. Inspector Hudson solved many crimes.

2. The caretaker saw different kinds of tourists.

3. Prince Vikram was near St. Paul's Cathedral.

4. Inspector Hudson caught many criminals.

5. Elvira Elliot worked a lot with Inspector Hudson.

6. They are looking for a loose stone.

The *caretaker* and Miss Elvira watched him excitedly.
"Well, I'll be damned!" the *caretaker* commented.

Then he suddenly looked up at the cross *remorsefully*.

"Sorry!" he apologized.

Elvira Elliot and the inspector were *crouching* down, examining the hole.

"It's empty, I'm afraid," said a disappointed Inspector Hudson. "Either nothing was put here, or it has been removed."

"What's gone?" the *caretaker* asked.

"*Nothing in particular*," the inspector answered.

By now the *caretaker* seemed very confused.

Inspector Hudson carefully put the loose stone back into position and stood up.

! *Übung 72: Setzen Sie die richtige Präposition ein!*
(away, up (2x), into, down (2x), from, at)

ÜBUNG 72

1. crouch _____   5. hide _____
2. mix _____   6. calm _____
3. run _____   7. stare _____
4. stand _____   8. bump _____

"Did you *by any chance* see anybody else here looking about?" the inspector asked.

The *caretaker* thought hard for a moment.

"Yes, there was! I mean a lot of people are interested in the altar, but that man from India…"

"Prince Vikram?" Miss Elliot questioned.

"Yes, exactly! Anyway the man from India was particularly interested in the altar. I remember he looked at it for ages. He also asked my permission to go up close to it."

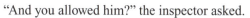

"And you allowed him?" the inspector asked.

"Yes, he was such a gentleman and so polite. One could never say no to a man like that."

"Really," said Inspector Hudson, looking over to his colleague *teasingly*. "Is that so?"

"Did you see him try to move the stones?" Elvira Elliot asked.

"No, no! He just walked around the altar a few times."

"When was that?" asked Inspector Hudson.

"Last night, just before closing time."

*Übung 73: Ergänzen Sie die Sätze mit **any** oder **some**!*

1. Miss Elliot and the inspector were at the cathedral to collect _____ evidence.

2. There were not _____ diamonds in the hole.

3. Prince Vikram was not alone; he had _____ people with him.

4. The caretaker does not have _____ idea what the prince was doing at the altar.

5. "Did Price Vikram walk around the altar at _____ point?" Miss Elliot asked.

6. _____ of the Crown Jewels had gone missing.

7. Inspector Hudson is tired. He would love to have _____ holidays.

"Was the cathedral as empty as this?" the inspector asked.

"Yes, more or less."

"Was the prince alone?"

"No, he had a very large and muscular *companion*."

"Probably one of his bodyguards," Miss Elliot said to Inspector Hudson.

He nodded, agreeing with what she said.

"Were you with the prince all of the time?" the inspector asked.

"No, not all the time. His *companion* had to go to the toilet, so I showed him where to go."

"And during that time Prince Vikram was alone?"

"Yes!"

The two *investigators* looked at each other, *acknowledging* they might be on to something.

They thanked the *caretaker* for his assistance and walked towards the cathedral's exit.

Übung 74: Lesen Sie weiter und ordnen Sie die Buchstaben in Klammern zu einem sinnvollen Wort!

"Maybe I was (1. thgri) _____ after all," Miss Elliot said excitedly. "Maybe the prince is our thief!"

"I don't know, Miss Elliot. It does seem *far-fetched*. (2. hapsrep) _____ he is just interested in altars."

"Well, he obviously likes them so (3. chum) _____ that he has been to St. Paul's Cathedral two days in a (4. owr) _____," she replied suspiciously.

The inspector opened his mouth to say (5. gomesihtn) _____.

"Let me finish," Miss Elvira *admonished* him.

Inspector Hudson (6. grughdes) _____.

"The diamond originally comes from (7. andiI) _____ and did not fall into British hands until the end of the nineteenth century. Perhaps the (8. creinp) _____ wants to take it back to where he believes it belongs? He does come from the same part of India where the (9. omandid) _____ got into British possession – I checked that out!"

Inspector Hudson still looked sceptical. They walked out of the church into the evening air. The inspector stopped and looked straight at Elvira Elliot.
"Okay, let's say he does have a motive and he stole the diamond. First question is: Did the prince pay Marc Drum and David Bucket to help him steal the diamond? Second question is: Did he kill Marc Drum after the robbery? If he did, he wasn't very careful, was he?"
"Why?"
"Because Prince Vikram made no secret of meeting Marc Drum. They met in the hotel lobby. Everybody saw them together."
"I guess you're right. Perhaps he feels very secure that nothing can happen to him. Or maybe Marc Drum wanted more money or something, got too greedy – he wasn't planning it in the beginning, but then had no other choice," Miss Elliot argued.
Inspector Hudson thought for a moment.

Übung 75: Welche Gegenteile gehören zusammen?

1. admonish
2. greed
3. be silent
4. assist
5. always
6. pull
7. empty

☐ moderation
☐ full
☐ push
☐ speak
☐ fight
☐ praise
☐ never

"Then why did he just kill Drum? He might as well have *got rid of* David Bucket while he was at it!" he said.

"Yes, but unlike David Bucket, Marc Drum knew his identity, because they had quite *evidently* met."

The inspector walked on. He was thinking hard about something. Elvira Elliot hurried along to catch up with him.

Inspector Hudson sighed.

"All right, maybe you have a point. And *apart from* that, we have no other *lead*. Let's go to the Savoy and question Prince Vikram – ask him what he was doing wandering around the altar shortly before closing time."

Elvira Elliot seemed very pleased. Inspector Hudson looked at her suspiciously.

"You're not making all of this seem plausible just so you can have another glance at pretty Prince Vikram?" he asked ironically.

"No, not at all," Miss Elliot answered. "It isn't always good to combine business and pleasure," she joked.

Inspector Hudson could not help but laugh.

"If Sir Reginald finds out we're after one of the Queen's friends, he's going to be *furious*!" the inspector exclaimed.

"Well, you can tell him it was my idea."

"I most certainly will," he answered. "That is, if you are wrong!" They both laughed and went towards the car.

Übung 76: Setzen Sie das passende Adjektiv ein!
(ancient, low, frightened, busy, helpful, difficult, wide)

1. A case that is hard to solve is _____.

2. A motorway with many lanes is _____.

3. A person who works very hard is _____.

4. A person who screams is _____.

5. A tower which is not very high is _____.

6. People who help you find a thief are _____.

7. A very old tree is _____.

8. Party Time

Elvira Elliot and Inspector Hudson walked into the lobby of the Savoy Hotel. Close by, near the bar, someone was playing the piano. The pleasant tune travelled throughout the lobby, *soothing* stressed-out businessmen and providing a pleasant welcome to new guests. The two *investigators* looked around to see if *by any chance* Prince Vikram happened to be in the hotel lobby, but he was nowhere to be seen. Inspector Hudson *shrugged* and looked over to the reception.

"No point in asking at the reception – looks like the same *bunch* that were working last time," the inspector said.

"Yes, they weren't very helpful the last time," Miss Elliot replied.
"I guess we'll just have to wait in the lobby and hope he turns up soon."
"We could leave a message that he has to report to Scotland Yard."
"Then he might get alarmed and leave the country before we have a chance to question him."
"I guess you're right," Miss Elliot said.
A waiter walked past them with a tray full of large exotic cocktails.
"Mmmm, do you fancy one of those?" Miss Elliot asked.
Inspector Hudson smiled.
"I think I'll go for some mineral water just now," he replied.
The inspector and Elvira Elliot were sitting at the bar. Inspector Hudson was drinking a mineral water. Elvira Elliot had a large alcoholic cocktail full of fruit. The bar was quite busy. Elegant women – their *precious* jewels *sparkling* in the light – were sitting beside men in hand-tailored suits. People were talking quietly. A man whispered something into a woman's ear. She laughed. The piano player was playing in the background.
"It's a bit like something out of a lifestyle magazine, isn't it?" said Elvira Elliot, as she sipped red juice through a straw.
"I don't know. I've never read a lifestyle magazine," Inspector Hudson answered.
Elvira Hudson laughed.
"What do you like to read in your free time?"
Inspector Hudson was about to answer when he saw Prince Vikram walk towards the reception followed by two of his bodyguards. They were carrying cases.
"Look, there's Prince Vikram!" he exclaimed.
The two *investigators* watched Prince Vikram take out his credit card.
"It looks as if he's checking out," Inspector Hudson said.

"Do you think he is *heading back* to India?"
"No idea!"
Prince Vikram took his credit card back and walked towards the exit.
"Let's follow him!" said the inspector. "Let's see if they are *heading* to the airport."

*Übung 77: Ergänzen Sie die If-Sätze mit **will**, **would** oder **would have**!*

1. If Inspector Hudson catches the prince, he _____ solve the case.

2. If Inspector Hudson found the diamond, he _____ solve the case.

3. If Inspector Hudson had caught the prince, he _____ solved the case.

4. Things _____ get easier if Inspector Hudson is on the right track.

5. It _____ get easier if Inspector Hudson can get a good night's sleep.

6. If the thief escaped, Inspector Hudson _____ be very angry.

Elvira Elliot and Inspector Hudson hid *neatly* behind a *bellboy* carrying cases and waited for them to pass. Then they walked carefully after them. They saw the prince and his *companions* get into a limousine. Miss Elliot and the inspector hurried towards the red sports car. They both got into the car and it shot off. They soon caught up with the limousine.

"They don't seem to be *heading for* the airport," Elvira Elliot said, as she *squealed* round a corner.

"No, they don't!" answered Inspector Hudson, a little nervously. "They seem to be *heading for* the South Bank."

"What could he be doing down there?" Elvira Elliot asked.

"Don't know, there are a number of important cultural buildings and institutions down that way." Inspector Hudson looked at his watch. "But everything will be more or less closed at this time," he continued.

> *Übung 78: Unterstreichen Sie das bekannte Sprichwort im folgenden Textabschnitt und übersetzen Sie es!*

Elvira Elliot shot through a red light to keep up with the limousine. Inspector Hudson closed his eyes. A car *approaching* from the other side of the crossing just missed them. The driver *tooted*. Inspector Hudson opened his eyes again.

"Well, that was close!"

"A miss is as good as a mile!" Miss Elvira said dryly and put her car into fifth gear.

"Yes, so they say!" the inspector replied uneasily.

By this time they had reached the London Borough of Lambeth, belonging to inner London.

"He's *heading* straight *for* the Jubilee Gardens," Inspector Hudson remarked.

In the distance they could see the London Eye – a huge modern version of Vienna's Prater wheel, which dominates the river skyline opposite the Parliament. It is the largest *observation wheel* in the world and stands 134 meters high on the western end of the Jubilee Gardens. Its lights *flashed* wildly, as if asking everyone to come and have a ride.

"Have you ever been up there?" Elvira Elliot asked the inspector.

"No, but I've heard you get the best view of London from there."

"Did you know that if you wish, you can book a whole *capsule*? Some people actually party all night in it," Elvira Elliot said.

"Sounds like fun," Inspector Hudson remarked ironically.

The London Eye was getting closer and closer.

"It seems to me that he is *heading* straight *for* that wheel," the inspector said in *astonishment*.

Übung 79: Lesen Sie weiter und vervollständigen Sie die Sätze mit dem passenden Wort!
(headed, gigantic, dressed, after, group, carrying, warmly)

Not long (1.) _____ this, the prince's limousine stopped very close to the entrance. Then the three men (2.) _____ for the London Eye. They were (3.) _____ the cases. Inspector Hudson and Miss Elliot followed them. They watched the prince meet up with a (4.) _____ of people who had obviously been waiting for him to arrive. They greeted the prince (5.) _____ and happily. Everybody was (6.)

_____ very well, and looked very *sophisticated*. In the background stood the massive wheel, which was turning steadily in the sky like a (7.) _____ UFO preparing to take off.

"It's amazing, isn't it?" Elvira Elliot said, her voice filled with wonder.
"Yes, it is", Inspector Hudson replied, "and it looks like Prince Vikram is boarding."
"Let's talk to him before he goes up in the air," the inspector said. "God knows when he'll be back down."
Miss Elliot and Inspector Hudson hurried along to catch up with the prince and his *companions*. They were all just climbing into the *capsule*, which looked like a miniature *spaceship*, when Inspector Hudson tapped the prince on the back.

> **!** *Übung 80: Lesen Sie weiter und unterstreichen Sie im Text die gegenteiligen Begriffe der Wörter in Klammern!*
> *(1. small 2. coldly 3. ugly 4. free-time 5. downwards 6. closed 7. loudly)*

Prince Vikram turned round.
"Inspector Hudson!" he said in great surprise. "What a *coincidence* to meet you here," Prince Vikram smiled warmly.
"Well, yes it is. We have a few questions, actually."
"Then why don't you and your beautiful colleague come for a ride?" Prince Vikram asked.
"Well, I don't know…" said the inspector.
"Oh, come on – mix business and pleasure."

Inspector Hudson looked at Elvira Elliot. She looked at him as if to say: Oh, why not!

"All right then!" Inspector Hudson said, and they all climbed *aboard*.

Soon after that, the egg-shaped *capsule* started to move upwards slowly. In the middle of the *capsule* was a built-in table. One of the bodyguards laid a case on top and opened it. The case was full of Champagne. Everybody cheered.

Inspector Hudson leant over to Elvira Elliot and said quietly to her, "So that's what he's got in the cases, drinks for his party."

"I know, and I thought he was off to India with the Kohinoor in one of the cases."

Champagne corks *popped* and loud disco music began to play out of a ghetto blaster. Prince Vikram came over to Miss Elliot and Inspector Hudson. He offered each of them a glass of Champagne. They *regretfully declined*, telling the prince they were still *on duty*.

"Still *on duty*, are you?" Prince Vikram asked with an ironical, sceptical undertone. "That means you probably have some more questions about the missing *Beefeater*?"

"I'm afraid he's no longer missing," said the inspector.

"Good, then he has probably *confirmed* that we met to talk about my film."

"No, I'm afraid not. Marc Drum is dead," Inspector Hudson replied.

"Dead!" the prince exclaimed. "Why, that's *awful*!"

"Yes, he drowned in the Thames!"

"Oh, dear!"

The prince hesitated for a minute. He was thinking about something and was looking out at the city below him.

Übung 81: *Ordnen Sie die Wörter auf der rechten Seite den Begriffen auf der linken zu!*

1. decline
2. probable
3. glance
4. hesitate
5. offer
6. pleasure
7. drown
8. awful

a) ☐ sink, go under, soak
b) ☐ pause, delay, falter
c) ☐ give, present, propose
d) ☐ glimpse, peek, look
e) ☐ likely, apparent, possible
f) ☐ terrible, bad, dreadful
g) ☐ delight, joy, bliss
h) ☐ refuse, reject, turn down

"Wait a minute; you don't think I have anything to do with his death, do you?"

Inspector Hudson did not say anything at first.

"That is *ridiculous*!" Prince Vikram exclaimed.

"Where were you on the night of the Tower robbery?" asked the inspector.

"*That's none of your business*!" said the prince, who was starting to get very annoyed. His whole gentlemanly style was beginning to *fade*.

"And what were you doing at the altar in St. Paul's Cathedral? Were you looking for anything in particular?" asked Elvira Elliot.

Prince Vikram downed his Champagne.

"I'll tell you something", he said, "your *accusations* are *ridiculous*. If you have any further questions, contact my lawyer. Also I ask you to leave my *capsule* as soon as we've gone round once – and now if you would excuse me!"

Prince Vikram turned away from them and moved towards a group of friends. The prince started laughing and talking as if the conversation with the police had never taken place.

*Übung 82: Vervollständigen Sie die Sätze mit **anywhere**, **nobody**, **anybody**, **nothing** oder **anything**!*

1. Prince Vikram says he has _____ to do with the robbery.

2. He believes the investigators do not have _____ that could prove his guilt.

3. The prince was not _____ near the Tower at the time of the theft.

4. His bodyguards normally did not let _____ near him.

5. The capsule was absolutely full. You couldn't say there was _____ in it.

6. Inspector Hudson did not say _____.

7. The prince acts as if _____ has happened.

"Well, that didn't go very well," remarked the inspector. "And we have no *evidence*, just some wild speculations."
"But he did react rather harshly, don't you think?" said Elvira Elliot.
"Yes, he did. And now we're stuck up here with this *bunch*!" the inspector complained.
"We might as well enjoy the view," Miss Elvira said, trying to *cheer* the inspector *up*.
"We might as well," the inspector sighed. "Our whole theory stands or falls on whether he has an alibi or not."

ÜBUNG 83

Übung 83: Bilden Sie Sätze mit dem Komparativ!

1. Prince Vikram/Inspector Hudson (rich)

   Prince Vikram is richer than Inspector Hudson.

2. tower/bridge (high)

   ___

3. London Eye/Prater Wheel (big)

   ___

4. Savoy/two-star hotel (expensive)

   ___

5. Westminster Abbey/Madame Tussaud's (old)

   ___

6. unknown thief/David Bucket (bad)

   ___

7. Elvira Elliot/Inspector Hudson (drive fast)

   ___

The inspector looked over at the prince.
"I mean, look at him. He's about 1.75m, *narrow-shouldered* and has dark brown eyes. For all we know it could be him, but it could also be someone else entirely. Can you think of anybody else who looks like that?"
"No, not at the moment," Elvira Elliot answered.
"Neither can I," said Inspector Hudson thoughtfully.

*Übung 84: Geben Sie die richtigen Formen von **to hit** mit **we** an!*

1. Einfache Gegenwart: _____
2. Verlaufsform der Gegenwart: _____
3. Einfache Vergangenheit: _____
4. Verlaufsform der Vergangenheit: _____
5. Perfekt: _____
6. Verlaufsform mit Perfekt: _____
7. Zukunft mit "going to" _____
8. Zukunft mit "will" _____

All of a sudden his mobile phone rang.
"Sergeant Wood?" the inspector said.
"Good evening, sir!" he answered
"What's up? Any news on that knife I gave you?"
"Yes, that's why I'm calling."
"And?"
"Well, as you *assumed,* it is a very *precious*, rare knife – it was made by a Japanese knife craftsman called Arishima Yoshimi about 60 years ago. Only three of these knives exist: One belongs to an American millionaire, one to a Japanese businessman and the last one belonged to a British major. The old man died a couple of years ago and the knife has been missing since."
"What was his name?"
"Brian Smith."
"I see. So Prince Vikram is definitely not the owner."
"I'm afraid not!"

"Were there any fingerprints on the knife?"
"No, just Mr and Mrs Moore's."
"Thought so!" Inspector Hudson sighed. "Well, thanks for calling."
"Goodbye!"
"Yes, goodbye!"

Übung 85: Welche Wörter gehören zusammen?

1. afraid
2. drive
3. finger
4. belong
5. true
6. gentle
7. fed
8. narrow
9. on

- [ ] to
- [ ] shouldered
- [ ] man
- [ ] up
- [ ] fast
- [ ] duty
- [ ] of
- [ ] prints
- [ ] story

The inspector put his mobile back into his pocket. He looked over at Prince Vikram, who was flirting with a pretty English girl.
"It's not his knife anyway," he said, nodding in the prince's direction.
"I can see our theory is falling apart more and more," Miss Elliot sighed.
"Looks like it."
"Who did the knives belong to?"
"Two guys who don't live *remotely* anywhere near Britain."
"And the third?"
"Belonged to some British major called Brian Smith."
"I see. We should check him out then."

"Unfortunately he's dead," Inspector Hudson explained.
"Oh, and the knife?"
"Well, it's obviously the knife we have."

Übung 86: Lesen Sie weiter und unterstreichen Sie die richtige Variante!

The wheel was slowing (1.) down/up. The *capsule* came to a halt. Prince Vikram signalled to one of his men that the two *investigators* had to leave. Elvira Elliot and Inspector Hudson could not wait to get (2.) out/away of the smoky, noisy *capsule*. They went towards the door, climbed out and (3.) stopped/started walking in the direction of the car.
"I'll have my men find out whether Brian Smith has any relatives – maybe a *Beefeater*."
"How did you come to that (4.) seclusion/conclusion?" Miss Elliot asked, *puzzled*.
"Perhaps we've been on the (5.) wrong/rong track all along. Perhaps more than one *Beefeater* was in on the robbery."
"But what does that have to do with Brian Smith?"
"Just a logical (6.) sought/thought: Brian Smith was a soldier. Soldiers' sons often become soldiers (7.) to/too, and you have to be a soldier to become a *Beefeater*."
"Oh, I see," said Miss Elliot, (8.) impressed/depressed. "It would seem (9.) causable/plausible if more than one was in on it – after all, it was a big coup and (10.) nothing/nobody was caught."
Inspector Hudson nodded.

"If one of the *Beefeaters* or guards is our masked robber, we need to find out which ones fit our limited description of the masked robber. We should also check out who was not *on duty* that night. However, we'll still have to verify Prince Vikram's alibi as soon as his lawyer gets it to us – I still don't think we should leave him off the hook. His behaviour certainly has been somewhat suspicious," the inspector said.

"And tomorrow I think we should pay Mrs Drum another visit," Elvira Elliot added.

"Yes, good idea, she should be out of hospital. But for now I need a good night's sleep."

"Same here!" Miss Elliot *yawned*. They got into the car and drove away.

9. Trapped

The next morning, Inspector Hudson was sitting in his office reading a book. He was waiting for Elvira Elliot to arrive so that they could drive out together to Mrs Drum's house.

Suddenly, Sir Reginald burst in and threw the morning newspaper onto the inspector's desk.

"Here. Look at this! I hate repeating myself, Inspector Hudson, but this whole investigation is getting out of hand," Sir Reginald said angrily.

The inspector calmly put his book down and looked at the newspaper *headline*. It read: "Is Indian Prince the Diamond Thief?" Below was a large picture of Prince Vikram.

"Can you explain this to me?" Sir Reginald asked crossly.

"No, not really," Inspector Hudson answered.

"Not really?" Sir Reginald exclaimed. "So tell me: how in heaven's name did this information *leak* to the papers? It's a scandal – I'll have the Queen herself on the phone next!"

Übung 87: Setzen Sie die Sätze ins Passiv!

1. Inspector Hudson caused the scandal.

   The scandal was caused by Inspector Hudson.

2. The thieves killed Marc Drum.

   _____

3. The inspector understands Sir Reginald's point.

   _____

4. Sir Reginald slammed the newspaper on the desk.

   _____

5. The journalist wrote a scandalous article.

   _____

6. The inspector put his mobile into his pocket.

   _____

Inspector Hudson sighed and explained to his *superior* the reasons why he and Miss Elliot had questioned Prince Vikram. After he had finished, Sir Reginald was no more amused than he had been to start with.

"I know there is hardly any *evidence* except that he met Marc Drum once and *scrutinized* the altar at St. Paul's Cathedral. However, it was just one *clue* we had to follow – police routine. But how the story got to the newspapers, I don't know," Inspector Hudson said.

"Well, I am going to call Prince Vikram and apologize to him personally. The poor man must be *devastated*. Do you know what news like this can do to a man's *reputation*?"

Übung 88: Enträtseln Sie die folgenden Definitionen!

1. a sharp, pointed object　　　　＿＿＿＿＿＿＿＿ (ifekn)

2. a female monarch　　　　　　＿＿＿＿＿＿＿＿ (enequ)

3. something which causes great outrage ＿＿＿＿＿＿＿ (anadlcs)

4. a noise of annoyance or relief ＿＿＿＿＿＿＿＿ (igsh)

5. to come to a stop　　　　　　＿＿＿＿＿＿＿＿ (lath)

6. on top of a newspaper article ＿＿＿＿＿＿＿＿ (leinaedh)

7. to interview someone　　　　＿＿＿＿＿＿＿＿ (euqnoits)

8. the London underground　　　＿＿＿＿＿＿＿＿ (ebtu)

"I'm sure he'll survive it", the inspector remarked *wearily*, "and I would like to state that he still is a *suspect*."
"And I would like to state that you leave the man alone!" Sir Reginald said *furiously*.
His face was red with anger. Without another word, he left the room. Just as Sir Reginald left, Miss Elliot arrived. He stormed past without saying hello to her.
"What was all that about?" she asked.
Inspector Hudson pointed at the newspaper.

Übung 89: Fügen Sie die Übersetzung der angegebenen Wörter ein!

"(1. kein Wunder) ＿＿＿＿＿＿＿＿＿＿ he was angry. I would like to know how that reached the papers."

"Maybe one of his party guests earned himself an extra pound or two," Inspector Hudson remarked (2. trocken) _____.

"Yes, perhaps! Has the prince's alibi been checked yet?"

"No, we're still waiting for a fax from his (3. Anwalt) _____."

"Oh, dear!" Miss Elliot (4. plötzlich) _____ exclaimed.

"What is it?"

"After reading the news, Prince Vikram might (5. versuchen) _____ to leave the country!"

"Well, we won't be able to stop (6. ihn) _____."

"And what if he is the thief and the (7. Mörder) _____?"

"Try and (8. erklären) _____ that one to Sir Reginald."

Elvira Elliot hurried over to Inspector Hudson's computer. She (9. suchte) _____ for the Savoy and wrote down the number. Then she picked up the phone and called the hotel.

"The Savoy Hotel, how may I help you?"
"Yes, good day!" said Elvira Elliot in a *fake posh* voice. "My name is Lady Fellowes. Could you put me through to Prince Vikram, please?"
"Sorry Madam, but Prince Vikram has already checked out this morning."
"Oh, has he now. Is he still in the hotel?"
"I am afraid that is all I can tell you, Madam."

"Well, it is rather important. He left his wallet at my house yesterday evening and I have to return it to him."

"Okay Madam, no problem. You can send it to the hotel. He's sitting in the tearoom. As far as I *am aware*, his flight does not leave until the afternoon."

"Thank you very much. You have been a great help. Goodbye!"

"Goodbye!"

Übung 90: Wie heißt der Satz auf Deutsch? Kreuzen Sie die richtige Übersetzung an!

1. There is hardly any evidence.
   a) ☐ Es gibt schwerwiegende Beweise.
   b) ☐ Es gibt harte Beweise.
   c) ☐ Es gibt kaum Beweise.

2. Is there any news about the knife?
   a) ☐ Gibt es irgendwelche Neuigkeiten zum Messer?
   b) ☐ Gibt es keine Nachrichten zum Messer?
   c) ☐ Gibt es Neuheiten zum Messer?

3. They are pretty close to solving the case.
   a) ☐ Sie sind hübsch darin, den Fall zu lösen.
   b) ☐ Sie sind ziemlich nah dran, den Fall zu lösen.
   c) ☐ Sie sind ziemlich nah dran, den Fall abzuschließen.

4. Prince Vikram was at the hotel.
   a) ☐ Prince Vikram war im Hotel.
   b) ☐ Prince Vikram war am Hotel.
   c) ☐ Prince Vikram war auf dem Hotel.

5. Miss Elliot cheered the inspector up.
   a) ☐ Miss Elliot jubelte den Inspektor an.
   b) ☐ Miss Elliot beklatschte den Inspektor.
   c) ☐ Miss Elliot munterte den Inspektor auf.

Elvira Elliot looked at Inspector Hudson and smiled.
"So what did you think of that?" she asked in her *fake posh* voice.
"I'm impressed!" the inspector replied.
"Prince Vikram is still at the hotel. We need to try and somehow prevent him from leaving the country until his innocence has been proven!"
"That sounds like a difficult one," Inspector Hudson said sceptically.
"I'll think of something – even if he just misses his plane today. That would give us at least a little more time. For all we know the Kohinoor diamond could be off to India today!"
"Okay, I see your point. You drive to the hotel and observe Prince Vikram. I'll go to Edith Drum and have another look around her *late* husband's office."
The two *investigators* hurried out of the office.

Übung 91: Unterstreichen Sie die Synonyme für die Ausdrücke in Klammern!
(1. wore 2. memorial service 3. upset 4. miserably 5. returned 6. found 7. walked by)

Edith Drum opened the door and let the inspector in. She was dressed in a black jumper and trousers. She looked very sad as she led Inspector Hudson to Marc Drum's office.

"Well, I'll leave you to it, Inspector. I am just in the middle of organizing my *late* husband's *funeral*."

"I do have some questions I would like to ask you though."

Edith Drum sighed. She looked very *distressed*.

"Can't that wait?" she asked sadly.

Inspector Hudson hesitated and looked at her.

"Of course it can," he said. "We can talk later."

Edith Drum went back downstairs. Inspector Hudson started looking through Marc Drum's things. After searching for a while, Inspector Hudson came across some photographs. They showed Marc Drum and his wife climbing up a mountain. Inspector Hudson laid the photographs down and walked out of Marc Drum's office. He passed the bedroom and looked in.

The bed wasn't made and the window was open. On a shelf beside the bed he saw a number of *trophies* of various sizes, won in gymnastic tournaments.

"Climbing, gymnastics," the inspector *mumbled under* his *breath*.

Inspector Hudson walked down the stairs. He found Mrs Drum in the kitchen. She was smoking a cigarette.

"Are you doing okay?" he asked her.

"I get by," she answered, blowing out the smoke. He looked at her standing there in her black outfit. He noticed that she had narrow shoulders and was quite tall for a woman.

"Did you use to do gymnastics?" Inspector Hudson asked *casually*.

"Yes, a bit, when I was younger. Why?"

"Just wondering," the inspector asked. "And climbing?"

"That was more Marc's passion, but I did go along with him occasionally."

"I see. I actually came down to ask you if I could use your bathroom." Inspector Hudson smiled politely.

"Of course, it's up the stairs and then the first door on the right."
"Thank you!"

Übung 92: Bilden Sie positive Sätze!

1. Prince Vikram didn't stay at the Savoy.

   Prince Vikram stayed at the Savoy.

2. His bodyguards weren't very strong.

3. Inspector Hudson disliked Miss Elliot.

4. Miss Elliot hates the way Inspector Hudson dresses.

5. Nobody knew who stole the Kohinoor diamond.

6. Mrs Drum doesn't have blue eyes.

7. Inspector Hudson didn't find Mrs Drum in the kitchen.

Inspector Hudson turned around and walked in the direction of the stairs.
"Oh, Inspector!" Edith Drum called after him. "Did you find anything interesting?" she asked.

"I'm not quite sure," he replied as he walked up the stairs.

Inspector Hudson went into the bathroom and closed the door.

"The description of the thief could fit, but Mrs Drum has blue eyes," he thought.

The inspector washed his hands. His eyes wandered around. Suddenly he saw a small white container.

"That's it! Contact lenses!" he exclaimed.

*Übung 93: Setzen Sie **to** oder **too** ein!*

1. Mrs Drum showed the inspector the way _____ the office.

2. Edith Drum was _____ distressed to have a normal conversation.

3. Inspector Hudson is trying _____ solve the crime.

4. Marc Drum used _____ live in the house _____.

5. Edith Drum did some climbing _____.

6. She told Inspector Hudson where _____ find the bathroom.

7. Inspector Hudson wanted _____ ask some questions.

Inspector Hudson took his phone out of his pocket and called Scotland Yard. It was ringing. Suddenly, the bathroom door opened.

"Put the phone down, Inspector!" Edith Drum said in a cold, hard voice.

Inspector Hudson looked up and saw through the reflection of the mirror that Edith Drum was pointing a gun at him. Someone on the other end of the phone line answered.

"I said put it down!" she *hissed*.

Inspector Hudson slowly put the phone down and turned around.

"You're the thief dressed in black!" Inspector Hudson said, raising his hands.

"Well observed, Watson!" she *mocked* him, taking the mobile phone from him.

"Now move into the office, slowly. And don't try any tricks or you're dead!"

Inspector Hudson walked into the office. He did not take his eyes off the weapon that Edith Drum was pointing at him.

Übung 94: Verwandeln Sie die Sätze in direkte Rede!

1. Edith Drum said she used to do gymnastics.

   "I used to do gymnastics."

2. She said she was in the middle of organizing her late husband's funeral.

3. Inspector Hudson asked where the bathroom was.

4. Elvira Elliot said she liked working with Inspector Hudson.

5. Sergeant Wood said he would like to be an inspector one day.

6. Edith Drum told Inspector Hudson to put down his phone.

"Sit down on the chair!" Edith Drum commanded.

Inspector Hudson sat down. Edith Drum got some climbing rope out of a drawer and tied him to the chair, all the time pointing the gun at him. After she had tied him up, she stepped a little way back from him.

"You really had us fooled," Inspector Hudson said.

Edith Drum smiled coldly.

"When I was young, I always dreamed of being an actress. It was a good show, wasn't it – all the worrying, the nervous breakdown."

"Yes, very convincing."

Edith Drum *bowed*.

"Thank you!" she said.

*Übung 95: Setzen Sie ein: **do** oder **make**?*

1. Inspector Hudson had to _____ a phone call.

2. Marc Drum could not _____ his wife happy.

3. Edith Drum had to _____ a lot of training before she stole the diamond.

4. She told Inspector Hudson to _____ exactly what she said.

5. By threatening Inspector Hudson, Mrs Drum was going to _____ things worse.

6. Sergeant Wood had to _____ some research to find out who the knife belonged to.

7. _____ as I tell you!

"So you actually killed your own husband?"
"Yes!"
"But why, when he obviously helped you?"
"He was a *wimp* and was in the way anyway," Edith Drum replied dismissively.
"In the way of what?"
The front door opened.
"Edith? Edith? Are you home?" said a man's voice from downstairs.
"I'm up here, dear!" Edith Drum called.
Craig Gunn *appeared* at the door. He looked *dumbfounded* as he saw what was going on. In disbelief he stared at the weapon Edith Drum was still pointing at the inspector.
"Oh, now I understand why your husband was in the way," Inspector Hudson remarked. "You started an affair with one of the Tower guards who just happened to be *on duty* the night of the robbery. He helped you as well, I *assume*?"
Edith Drum nodded.
"What on earth are you doing!" exclaimed Craig Gunn. "Have you gone totally mad?"
"No, dear, just *playing it safe*," she replied *casually*. She did not even look at her lover but kept her eyes fixed on Inspector Hudson.
"But he's a policeman. You're making things worse and worse. What are you going to do, kill him?"
"Why not, he's the only one who knows."
"You can't just kill a policeman and expect to get away with it. They'll hunt us like foxes!" Craig Gunn kept running his fingers through his hair. Obviously, he was very nervous.
"Oh, don't be such a *wimp*!" Edith Drum *admonished* her lover.
Then, Edith Drum pulled back the *trigger*.

Übung 96: Wählen Sie die richtige Variante!

1. Edith Drum spoke _____.

   a) cold   b) coldly

2. Inspector Hudson answered _____.

   a) calm   b) calmly

3. Marc Drum was _____ killed.

   a) brutally   b) brutal

4. Craig Gunn spoke in a _____ tone.

   a) hysterical   b) hysterically

5. Inspector Hudson was in _____ trouble.

   a) many   b) a lot of

6. Edith Drum was _____ prepared.

   a) good   b) well

7. It couldn't really get any _____.

   a) badder   b) worse

At the same time, Elvira Elliot was at the Savoy Hotel observing Prince Vikram, who was sitting in the tearoom with his bodyguards. They were joking and playing cards. Miss Elliot's phone rang. It was Sergeant Wood.

"Well, hello Sergeant, to what do I *owe* the pleasure of you calling me for a change?"

"Is Inspector Hudson with you? I must speak to him immediately!" the sergeant exclaimed.

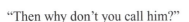

"Then why don't you call him?"
"I can't reach him. His mobile is off."
"Where is he?"
"He's at Edith Drum's house," Elvira Elliot answered.
"Oh!" said the sergeant in a worried voice.
"Why, what is it?"
"I just found out who Major Brian Smith *is related to*."
"Who?"
"He's Edith Drum's father – her *maiden name* was Smith!"
"That means she could be our man…erm…I mean woman!" exclaimed Elvira Elliot.
"Exactly!"
"Oh, I'm so stupid," Miss Elliot said, annoyed at herself. "Here I am watching an Indian prince playing cards with two gorillas!"

Übung 97: Wie lautet das Wort auf Englisch?

1. Mädchenname _____
2. scherzen _____
3. verblüfft _____
4. sofort _____
5. Raub _____
6. vornehm _____
7. vermuten _____
8. ermahnen _____
9. Mobiltelefon _____
10. Abzug (Waffe) _____
11. sich verbeugen _____
12. beiläufig _____

"There's something else I wanted to tell the inspector. Prince Vikram has a *cast-iron* alibi. He was dining with Lady Chatto – the only daughter of the *late* Princess Margaret."

"Well, that's a *firm* alibi." Miss Elliot said as she rushed out of the hotel, nearly knocking over the *bellboy*.

"Yes, there were over thirty people at the dinner party."

"Why didn't he just say so in the first place?" exclaimed the insurance *investigator*.

"I guess we'll see each other at Mrs Drum's – and hurry up, Inspector Hudson might be in danger!"

"Yes, see you there!"

Elvira Elliot hurried out of the hotel lobby.

Übung 98: *Sind diese Sehenswürdigkeiten in London? Markieren Sie mit richtig ✔ oder falsch – !*

1. Big Ben ☐
2. British Museum ☐
3. No. 10 Downing Street ☐
4. David Livingstone House ☐
5. Shakespeare's House ☐
6. Tate Modern ☐
7. Brick Lane Market ☐

Edith Drum was still pointing the gun at Inspector Hudson.

"Edith, darling, please, let's just pack our stuff and get out of here!" Craig Gunn *pleaded*.

Edith Drum swung the gun around and pointed it at her lover.

"Would you please just shut up, Craig!" she said in an annoyed voice.

Craig Gunn put his arms up defensively.

"Okay, okay, you're the boss!"

Edith Drum turned around again and pointed the gun back at

Inspector Hudson. She smiled *wickedly* and took a step forward. "That's right, I'm the boss!"

"So you planned it?" the inspector asked.

"Yes, every single step."

"How did you manage to persuade your husband to help you?"

"To keep the answers simple", replied Edith Drum, "love makes people blind."

"So does hate," Inspector Hudson remarked.

Edith Drum *frowned*. "Do you think so, Inspector? I think hate gives you *incredible* power, makes you do things you never thought possible."

"Like kill a man," the inspector remarked dryly.

"That's one example! Love, on the other hand, just makes you weak."

Edith Drum looked over to Craig Gunn. By this time, he seemed very confused.

Übung 99: Lesen Sie weiter und unterstreichen Sie im folgenden Abschnitt alle neun Verben im Simple Past!

"Edith, what are you talking about?" he said in a *devastated* voice.

"Shut up!" she *barked*.

"Why the Kohinoor diamond?"

"There was no particular reason, but it is very beautiful, don't you think?"

Edith Drum took the diamond out of a *belt bag* she had tied around her waist and looked at it. It *sparkled* in the light.

Elvira Elliot arrived at Edith Drum's house. Sergeant Wood had not arrived yet. She looked in the living room window, but could not see anything. She carefully *approached* the door.

Back in the house Edith Drum was still admiring the diamond. Craig Gunn suddenly jumped on her and tried to take the gun off her. However, Edith Drum was faster and shot a bullet into his stomach.

"Argghhhh!" he cried. Elvira Elliot *started* as she heard the man's scream.

"Oh, God!" she *mumbled* as she *fumbled* a small, thin tool out of her bag. She put it into the lock.

Craig Gunn was lying on the floor *bleeding*, holding his stomach. He was in great *agony*. Inspector Hudson tried very hard to get up off the chair, but he was tied too tightly. He just *toppled over* and fell to the ground.

Edith Drum turned her attention to the inspector.

"Now it's your turn", she said coldly.

She pulled back the *trigger*. Just as she was about to shoot Inspector Hudson, Elvira Elliot *tiptoed* into the room with a vase in her hand. She *smashed* it over Edith Drum's head. She screamed and fell over. The gun fell out of her hand and onto the floor. Elvira Elliot picked it up.

Edith Drum was lying on the floor holding her head. She was *moaning*. Miss Elliot *bent down* and untied the inspector.

"Well, I'm pleased to see you, Miss Elliot," he said relieved.

"That's the first time I've ever heard you say that," she smiled.

Inspector Hudson got to his feet. He took the gun from Miss Elliot and pointed it at Edith Drum, who was still holding her head. The inspector stepped over to Craig Gunn.

"We'd better call an ambulance!"

Outside, police sirens could be heard that were getting closer.

"That will be Sergeant Wood with the cavalry," said Elvira Elliot.

"I bet he'll be disappointed to have missed out on all the action," Inspector Hudson remarked.

Übung 100: Welches Wort ist das „schwarze Schaf"?

1. command, order, obey, demand
2. posh, poor, noble, high-born
3. over, under, above, more than
4. point, tip, end, bottom
5. wicked, kind, furious, evil
6. dumbfounded, amazed, knowing, astonished
7. shoot, bullet, trigger, barrel

A little later, the inspector and Miss Elliot were standing outside the house. Craig Gunn was being carried into an ambulance and Edith Drum sat in a police car.
"It's funny, that," Elvira Elliot said thoughtfully.
"What's funny?" Inspector Hudson asked.
"That the diamond actually lived up to its *reputation* once again."
"What do you mean?"
"Well, you know it has still not been bought or sold and, as usual, it has left a trail of *greed*, murder, *misfortune* and unhappiness behind it."
"You're not getting *superstitious*, are you?"
"No, but it is strange how fate has repeated itself after so many thousands of years."
"Hard to imagine that a thing so beautiful can cause so much *harm*," the inspector said. He paused and sighed.
"Maybe I should keep it at home for a while and see what happens," he joked.
"You most certainly won't!" Miss Elliot exclaimed, *snatching* the diamond out of his hand. "It's going straight to the Tower of London where it belongs – to be locked up out of everybody's reach."
Inspector Hudson *shrugged*. He waved a constable over. He had a

small iron case with him. Elvira Elliot put the diamond into it.

"Contact Sir Reginald and have him send a security van over to pick up the diamond."

"Yes, Sir!" said the constable. He walked away and gave the diamond to Sergeant Wood. Elvira Elliot and Inspector Hudson watched this happen.

"What a morning, eh?" Inspector Hudson exclaimed. "I didn't even get to finish my tea."

"Have you any plans, Inspector?" Miss Elliot asked.

"Plans?"

"I mean, do you feel like a cup of tea?"

"Yes, why not!"

"Good! I know this quiet place just down the road."

They walked towards their cars.

"I'll drive myself this time, if you don't mind," Inspector Hudson said.

"No problem, Inspector!" Miss Elliot teased him.

She started running towards her car.

"Last one there pays!" she grinned as she opened her car door.

Inspector Hudson smiled and unlocked his car unhurriedly.

"I *owe* you one anyway!" he shouted back.

However, Elvira Elliot did not hear this – she was already *speeding* up the road.

THE END

Abschlusstest

Übung 1: Welche Gegenteile gehören zusammen?

1. slow down
2. weak
3. never
4. stand
5. towards
6. scream
7. grab

- [ ] let go
- [ ] always
- [ ] whisper
- [ ] strong
- [ ] hurry
- [ ] walk
- [ ] away from

Übung 2: Welcher Satz enthält die richtige Übersetzung?

1. David Bucket war auch am Tower.
   a) [ ] David Bucket was at the Tower to.
   b) [ ] David Bucket was at the Tower too.

2. Die Polizei konnte sie nicht aufhalten.
   a) [ ] The police could not stop them.
   b) [ ] The police could not stop themselves.

3. Sergeant Wood und Inspector Hudson trafen sich.
   a) [ ] Sergeant Wood and Inspector Hudson meeted.
   b) [ ] Sergeant Wood and Inspector Hudson met.

4. Elvira Elliot fuhr gerade mit dem Auto.
   a) [ ] Elvira Elliot drives the car.
   b) [ ] Elvira Elliot was driving the car.

5. Sergeant Wood hat ihnen schon sehr oft geholfen.
   a) ☐ Sergeant Wood helped them a lot already.
   b) ☐ Sergeant Wood has helped them a lot.

Übung 3: Wie heißt das Simple Past der folgenden Verben?

1. hear _____
2. come _____
3. do _____
4. make _____
5. swim _____
6. walk _____
7. lay _____
8. hide _____
9. wear _____
10. dab _____

Übung 4: Bilden Sie sinnvolle Phrasal Verbs!

1. crouch   ☐ out
2. call   ☐ down
3. mix   ☐ in
4. fill   ☐ off
5. back   ☐ by
6. drop   ☐ on
7. eat   ☐ up

Übung 5: Setzen Sie, wenn notwendig, den richtigen Artikel ein!

1. The thief will go to _____ prison.

2. Sir Reginald was in _____ bad mood.

3. Miss Elliot hadn't talked to the inspector for half _____ hour.

4. Inspector Hudson got out of _____ bed.

5. The Kohinoor diamond was no longer in _____ Tower.

6. David Bucket got more than just _____ few hundred pounds.

7. Inspector Hudson tried to get _____ overview of everything that happened.

Übung 6: Simple Present oder Verlaufsform? Unterstreichen Sie die richtige Form des Präsens!

1. Mrs Drum plays/is playing cards at the moment.
2. It snows/is snowing outside.
3. David Bucket never knows/is knowing what to do.
4. Miss Elliot usually travels/is travelling by car.
5. Inspector Hudson goes/is going home now.
6. Where does/is doing Marc Drum stay?

Übung 7: Welche Synonyme gehören zusammen?

1. boat	☐ force
2. enquiry	☐ proceed
3. huge	☐ innocent
4. funeral	☐ investigation
5. blameless	☐ ship
6. advance	☐ enormous
7. might	☐ memorial service

Übung 8: Wie lauten die typischen Londoner Sehenswürdigkeiten? Ordnen Sie die Buchstaben zu einem sinnvollen Wort!

1. yee nnoodl   _____
2. gib neb   _____
3. hmagnibcku lapace _____
4. retsnimestw   _____
5. ts aulps lardehtac _____
6. eeilbuj senrdag   _____
7. emamda sduatsus   _____
8. retwo dregib   _____

Übung 9: Setzen Sie das passende Adjektiv bzw. Adverb ein!
(well, helpful, safe, abruptly, ancient, good, high, harmless)

1. Inspector Hudson did very _____.
2. The tower was very _____.
3. Sergeant Wood was a _____ man.
4. The Tower of London is not old, it is _____.
5. The thief dressed in black was anything but _____.
6. Miss Elliot braked _____.
7. Buckingham Palace is a _____ place.
8. Edith Drum is not a _____ person.

Lösungen

Übung 1: 1. was 2. got 3. went 4. heard 5. fell 6. came 7. did 8. ate 9. let 10. said
Übung 2: 1. along 2. archway 3. think 4. guard 5. direction 6. escort 7. answer
Übung 3: 1. car 2. armed 3. guard 4. lantern 5. money 6. shoot 7. disappointed 8. happy Lösung: ceremony
Übung 4: 1. hurry/slow down 2. shout/whisper 3. cover/uncover 4. nervous/calm 5. strong/weak 6. keep/give 7. pull/push 8. light/heavy 9. friend/enemy 10. reply/ask
Übung 5: 1. helpful 2. exhausted 3. clever 4. strange 5. funny 6. good
Übung 6: 1. removed 2. placed 3. covered 4. propped 5. knocked 6. frowned
Übung 7: 1. Inspector Hudson looked forward to reading his book. 2. Inspector Hudson wore his pyjamas. 3. The thieves stole the Kohinoor diamond. 4. Miss Paddington tried to listen to the telephone conversation. 5. Inspector Hudson forgot to put on his shoes.
Übung 8: 1. nobody 2. his 3. sat 4. bright 5. think 6. far 7. blood 8. ambulance 9. socks 10. later
Übung 9: 1. – 2. The 3. a 4. an 5. – 6. the 7. – 8. the
Übung 10: 1. That is very impressive. 2. They walked towards the glass case. 3. Inspector Hudson admired the jewels. 4. Sir Reginald smiled triumphantly. 5. There were almost no witnesses. 6. Inspector Hudson looked pensively around the room. 7. Sir Reginald shrugged.
Übung 11: 1. Where 2. which 3. What 4. Who 5. Whose 6. Which 7. Why
Übung 12: 1. exited 2. walked 3. diamond 4. special 5. shrugged 6. speeded 7. pleased
Übung 13: 1. on 2. over 3. in 4. on 5. to 6. under 7. onto
Übung 14: 1. danger 2. miserable 3. thorny 4. alert 5. loads 6. argue 7. excess
Übung 15: 1. he isn't 2. they aren't 3. we won't 4. she didn't 5. it can't 6. she wouldn't 7. we haven't 8. they shouldn't
Übung 16: 1. called 2. He 3. I 4. interestedly 5. no 6. say 7. Calm 8. doing
Übung 17: 1. ask/inquire 2. innocent/blameless 3. exclaim/shout 4. close/shut 5. accomplice/assistant 6. pull/heave 7. understand/comprehend 8. force/might 9. proceed/advance 10. rough/violent
Übung 18: 1. much 2. much 3. many 4. many 5. much 6. many
Übung 19: 1. gently 2. thoughtfully 3. uneasily 4. harmlessly 5. safely 6. roughly 7. abruptly 8. mysteriously
Übung 20: 1. falsch 2. falsch 3. richtig 4. richtig 5. falsch 6. richtig 7. richtig
Übung 21: 1. arrived, arrived 2. run, ran 3. hide, hidden 4. made, made 5. keep, kept 6. shine, shone 7. thought, thought 8. wear, wore
Übung 22: 1. bellboy 2. joyride 3. hotel lobby 4. police badge 5. bookshelf 6. old-fashioned 7. typewriter
Übung 23: 1. Uhr, beobachten 2. Uniform, gleich 3. Ring, anrufen/läuten 4. Hand, geben 5. meines, Mine 6. Muse, grübeln

Übung 24: 1. waved 2. approached 3. inquired 4. generous 5. usual 6. point 7. eagerly

Übung 25: 1. Miss Elliot always drives fast. 2. Suddenly she saw the bellboy. 3. Inspector Hudson and Elvira Elliot just walked into the hotel. 4. Prince Vikram had just left. 5. Inspector Hudson should probably have asked the bellboy first.

Übung 26: 1. They walked outside. 2. It was a very modern building. 3. It was a very cheap copy. 4. They could see land in the distance. 5. It was like a rainbow.

Übung 27: 1. me 2. them 3. his 4. mine 5. him 6. your, mine

Übung 28: 1. Inspector Hudson would never let Miss Elliot drive his car. 2. Elvira Elliot would never admit that she drives too fast. 3. Inspector Hudson would never find the Whispering Gallery on his own. 4. Prince Vikram would never leave the house without his turban. 5. Sir Reginald would really like to catch the thief. 6. Miss Elliot would always work together with the inspector.

Übung 29: 1. cathedral 2. pillar 3. Renaissance 4. aisle 5. altar 6. nave 7. caretaker

Übung 30: 1. rang 2. answered 3. is 4. found 5. have checked 6. seems 7. seeing 8. meeting 9. are trying 10. know

Übung 31: 1. herself 2. himself 3. themselves 4. yourself 5. ourselves 6. itself

Übung 32: 1. brakes 2. tyres 3. heart attack 4. people 5. store 6. glimpse 7. gem

Übung 33: 1. street 2. borough 3. car 4. toot 5. square 6. shop 7. residential 8. hotel 9. Tower of London

Übung 34: 1. sparkling 2. talk 3. matter 4. gracefully 5. private 6. accompany

Übung 35: 1. reverse 2. finally/eventually 3. police badge 4. closed 5. unreliable 6. opening hours 7. enter 8. to bow 9. suspect

Übung 36: 1. longer, longest 2. deeper, deepest 3. nicer, nicest 4. more helpful, most helpful 5. narrower, narrowest 6. more exhausted, most exhausted 7. worse, worst 8. more comfortable, most comfortable

Übung 37: 1. ago 2. since 3. ago 4. for 5. since 6. for 7. for

Übung 38: 1. richtig 2. falsch 3. richtig 4. richtig 5. falsch 6. falsch

Übung 39: 1. connection 2. proudly 3. sounds 4. stops 5. hesitated 6. clues 7. solve

Übung 40: 1. standing 2. never 3. (very) small 4. bored 5. loves 6. towards 7. difficult

Übung 41: 1. Go! 2. Stop her/them! 3. Don't tell him! 4. Stop it! 5. Leave me alone! 6. Stay here!

Übung 42: 1. They were staying at a two-star hotel on Piccadilly Circus. 2. Yes, the underground was near the hotel. 3. They think Mr and Mrs Moore can help because Mr Moore filmed during the robbery at the Tower. 4. Yes, it was the same person. 5. A knife fell out of his pocket. 6. No, he didn't manage to steal the tape. 7. The Moores took the Piccadilly Line and the Circle Line.

Übung 43: 1. b 2. a 3. c 4. b 5. a

Übung 44: 1. picked 2. asked 3. thought 4. laughed 5. knew 6. teased 7. tried 8. walked 9. inserted 10. swallowed 11. pulled
Übung 45: 1. disregard 2. three 3. why 4. terrible 5. good 6. day 7. path
Übung 46: 1. real/false 2. hold/let go 3. fast-forward/rewind 4. miss/hit 5. clear/vague 6. whisper/scream 7. record/play
Übung 47: triumphantly, exactly, calmly, hard, disapprovingly, reproachfully
Übung 48: 1. will 2. are going to 3. is going to 4. will 5. are going to 6. am going to
Übung 49: 1. we are taking 2. we are preferring 3. we are travelling 4. we are lying 5. we are running 6. we are humming
Übung 50: 1. bald 2. towards 3. asked 4. long 5. sure 6. living 7. hope 8. late 9. good
Übung 51: 1. pressure 2. publicity 3. ringing 4. secretary 5. investigation 6. relieved 7. evidence 8. disbelief
Übung 52: 1. during 2. Last 3. ago 4. last 5. ago 6. during
Übung 53: 1. who 2. which 3. who 4. – 5. who 6. whose
Übung 54: 1. half past six 2. ten past ten 3. (a) quarter past three 4. twenty-five to nine 5. (a) quarter to one 6. five to eight 7. five past five
Übung 55: 1. remarcked (remarked) 2. collegue (colleague) 3. stoped (stopped) 4. quite (quiet) 5. here (hear) 6. wispered (whispered)
Übung 56: 1. would he 2. wouldn't she 3. wasn't she 4. isn't he 5. hasn't she 6. can't he 7. didn't he 8. won't they
Übung 57: 1. sneak 2. opposite 3. crashed 4. dashing 5. bumped 6. Near 7. heading
Übung 58: 1. sitting 2. see 3. asked 4. entered 5. going 6. exclaimed 7. believe 8. insisted
Übung 59: 1. groß 2. groß 3. – 4. – 5. groß 6. groß 7. –
Übung 60: 1. he does 2. he is doing 3. he did 4. he was doing 5. he has done 6. he has been doing 7. he is going to do 8. he will do
Übung 61: 1. the 2. – 3. a 4. – 5. the 6. the 7. a 8. –
Übung 62: 1. bodies 2. rivers 3. wives 4. busses 5. sheep 6. days 7. women drivers 8. knives 9. boxes 10. policemen
Übung 63: 1. Where 2. Who 3. Whose 4. Which 5. Why 6. What 7. Whom 8. Where
Übung 64: 1. Inspector Hudson arrived at the crime scene that/which was near the Thames. 2. They fought their way through curious spectators, who were in the way. 3. The Tower, which was close to the bridge, could be seen in the distance. 4. The body was found near the Thames, which was not good news. 5. Inspector Reid, who was working in the distance, could see them coming. 6. They nearly bumped into Sergeant Wood, who was holding a cup of coffee.
Übung 65: 1. stroked away 2. smiled (back) at 3. looked down 4. swollen up 5. looked away 6. pulling together 7. weighed down
Übung 66: 1. by 2. in 3. at 4. from 5. in 6. for 7. after 8. to
Übung 67: 1. nervous 2. murderer 3. colleagues 4. spectator 5. hesitate 6. accomplice 7. stretch Lösung: suspect
Übung 68: 1. falsch 2. falsch 3. falsch 4. richtig 5. richtig 6. falsch 7. falsch

Übung 69: 1. is calling 2. drives 3. believes 4. is having 5. does not help 6. says, leaves

Übung 70: 1. cathedral/church 2. ship/boat 3. large/huge 4. enter/go into 5. understand/comprehend 6. investigation/enquiry 7. inside/within

Übung 71: 1. Inspector Hudson has solved many crimes. 2. The caretaker has seen different kinds of tourists. 3. Prince Vikram has been near St. Paul's Cathedral. 4. Inspector Hudson has caught many criminals. 5. Elvira Elliot has worked a lot with Inspector Hudson. 6. They have been looking for a loose stone.

Übung 72: 1. crouch down 2. mix up 3. run away 4. stand up 5. hide from 6. calm down 7. stare at 8. bump into

Übung 73: 1. some 2. any 3. some 4. any 5. any 6. some 7. some

Übung 74: 1. right 2. Perhaps 3. much 4. row 5. something 6. shrugged 7. India 8. prince 9. diamond

Übung 75: 1. admonish/praise 2. greed/moderation 3. be silent/speak 4. assist/fight 5. always/never 6. pull/push 7. empty/full

Übung 76: 1. difficult 2. wide 3. busy 4. frightened 5. low 6. helpful 7. ancient

Übung 77: 1. will 2. would 3. would have 4. will 5. will 6. would

Übung 78: A miss is as good as a mile. = Knapp daneben ist auch vorbei.

Übung 79: 1. after 2. headed 3. carrying 4. group 5. warmly 6. dressed 7. gigantic

Übung 80: 1. small/great 2. coldly/warmly 3. ugly/beautiful 4. free-time/business 5. downwards/upwards 6. closed/opened 7. loudly/quietly

Übung 81: 1. h 2. e 3. d 4. b 5. c 6. g 7. a 8. f

Übung 82: 1. nothing 2. anything 3. anywhere 4. anybody 5. nobody 6. anything 7. nothing

Übung 83: 1. Prince Vikram is richer than Inspector Hudson. 2. The tower is higher than the bridge. 3. The London Eye is bigger than the Prater Wheel. 4. The Savoy is more expensive than a two-star hotel. 5. Westminster Abbey is older than Madame Tussaud's. 6. The unknown thief is worse than David Bucket. 7. Elvira Elliot drives faster than Inspector Hudson.

Übung 84: 1. we hit 2. we are hitting 3. we hit 4. we were hitting 5. we have hit 6. we have been hitting 7. we are going to hit 8. we will hit

Übung 85: 1. afraid of 2. drive fast 3. fingerprints 4. belong to 5. true story 6. gentleman 7. fed up 8. narrow-shouldered 9. on duty

Übung 86: 1. down 2. out 3. started 4. conclusion 5. wrong 6. thought 7. too 8. impressed 9. plausible 10. nobody

Übung 87: 1. The scandal was caused by Inspector Hudson. 2. Marc Drum was killed by the thieves. 3. Sir Reginald's point is understood by the inspector. 4. The newspaper was slammed on the desk by Sir Reginald. 5. A scandalous article was written by the journalist. 6. The mobile was put into his pocket by the inspector.

Übung 88: 1. knife 2. queen 3. scandal 4. sigh 5. halt 6. headline 7. question 8. tube

Übung 89: 1. No wonder 2. dryly 3. lawyer 4. suddenly 5. try 6. him 7. murderer 8. explain 9. searched
Übung 90: 1. c 2. a 3. b 4. a 5. c
Übung 91: 1. was dressed in 2. funeral 3. distressed 4. sadly 5. went back 6. came across 7. passed
Übung 92: 1. Prince Vikram stayed at the Savoy. 2. His bodyguards were very strong. 3. Inspector Hudson liked Miss Elliot. 4. Miss Elliot likes the way Inspector Hudson dresses. 5. Everybody/Somebody knew who stole the Kohinoor diamond. 6. Mrs Drum has blue eyes. 7. Inspector Hudson found Mrs Drum in the kitchen.
Übung 93: 1. to 2. too 3. to 4. to, too 5. too 6. to 7. to
Übung 94: 1. "I used to do gymnastics." 2. "I am in the middle of organizing my late husband's funeral." 3. "Where is your bathroom, please?" 4. "I like working with Inspector Hudson." 5. "I would like to be an inspector one day." 6. "Put your phone down!"
Übung 95: 1. make 2. make 3. do 4. do 5. make 6. do 7. Do
Übung 96: 1. b 2. b 3. a 4. a 5. b 6. b 7. b
Übung 97: 1. maiden name 2. joke 3. dumbfounded 4. immediately 5. robbery 6. posh 7. assume 8. admonish 9. mobile 10. trigger 11. bow 12. casually
Übung 98: 1. in London 2. in London 3. in London 4. nicht in London 5. nicht in London 6. in London 7. in London
Übung 99: 1. barked 2. was 3. took 4. looked 5. sparkled 6. arrived 7. looked 8. could (not) 9. approached
Übung 100: 1. obey 2. poor 3. under 4. bottom 5. kind 6. knowing 7. shoot

Lösungen Abschlusstest

Übung 1: 1. slow down/hurry 2. weak/strong 3. never/always 4. stand/walk 5. towards/away from 6. scream/whisper 7. grab/let go
Übung 2: 1. b 2. a 3. b 4. b 5. b
Übung 3: 1. heard 2. came 3. did 4. made 5. swam 6. walked 7. laid 8. hid 9. wore 10. dabbed
Übung 4: 1. crouch down 2. call on 3. mix up 4. fill in 5. back off 6. drop by 7. eat out
Übung 5: 1. – 2. a 3. an 4. – 5. the 6. a 7. an
Übung 6: 1. is playing 2. is snowing 3. knows 4. travels 5. is going 6. does
Übung 7: 1. boat/ship 2. enquiry/investigation 3. huge/enormous 4. funeral/memorial service 5. blameless/innocent 6. advance/proceed 7. might/force
Übung 8: 1. London Eye 2. Big Ben 3. Buckingham Palace 4. Westminster 5. St. Paul's Cathedral 6. Jubilee Gardens 7. Madame Tussaud's 8. Tower Bridge
Übung 9: 1. well 2. high 3. helpful 4. ancient 5. harmless 6. abruptly 7. safe 8. good

Glossar

fam umgangssprachlich
fig bildlich
pl Plural
v Verb

aboard	an Bord
abundance	Überfluss
accompany *v*	begleiten
accomplice	Komplize/Komplizin
accusation	Anschuldigung
acknowledge *v*	bestätigen, anerkennen
admonish *v*	ermahnen
affectionately	liebevoll
aggravated	gereizt, verärgert
agony	großer Schmerz
air raid	Luftangriff
aisle	Gang (zwischen Sitzbänken etc.)
alleged	angeblich, vorgeblich
A miss is as good as a mile.	Knapp daneben ist auch vorbei.
ancient	sehr alt; altertümlich
anxiously	ängstlich, beunruhigt
apart from	abgesehen von
appear *v*	auftauchen, erscheinen; scheinen
approach	Zugang
approach *v*	nahen, sich annähern
archway	Bogengang, gewölbter Eingang
armed	bewaffnet
assume *v*	vermuten, annehmen
astonishment	Überraschung
audible	hörbar

awful	furchtbar
babbling	plappernd
badge	Dienstmarke, Abzeichen
bark *v*	hier: jmdn. anherrschen; bellen
barracks	Kaserne
be (was, been) *v* **all ears** *fig*	ganz Ohr sein *fig*
be (was, been) *v* **(un)aware (of something)**	sich etwas (nicht) bewusst sein
be (was, been) *v* **capable of**	im Stande sein zu; können
be (was, been) *v* **in touch**	hier: sich melden; mit jemandem in Verbindung sein
be (was, been) *v* **of assistance**	hilfreich sein, behilflich sein
be (was, been) *v* **related to**	verwandt sein mit
be (was, been) *v* **startled**	erschrecken
beam	Lichtstrahl
beam *v*	(an)strahlen
Beat it! *fam*	Hau ab! *fam*
Beefeater	Wärter im Tower of London, königlicher Leibgardist
bellboy	Hotelpage
belongings *pl*	Eigentum, Sachen
belt bag	Gürteltasche
bend (bent, bent) *v* **(down)**	beugen; sich bücken
blade	Klinge
blazing	lodernd, flammend
bleeding	blutend
blind	hier: Blende, Rollo; blind
blunt	stumpf
bonnet	Mütze
boundary	Begrenzung, Grenze
bow *v*	sich verbeugen
bravery	Tapferkeit
briskly	rasch, flott

brush *v* **off**	abstauben, abbürsten
bump *v* **into**	zusammenstoßen
bunch (of people) *fam*	Haufen, Gruppe (von Menschen)
by (any) chance	zufällig, durch Zufall
capsule	hier: Gondel; Kapsel
caretaker	Hausmeister
carry *v* **on**	weitermachen
cast-iron	hier: lückenlos; gusseisern
casually	nebenbei, beiläufig
cat of prey	Raubkatze
catch *v* **someone's eye**	jemandes Blick/Aufmerksamkeit auf sich ziehen
Ceremony of the Keys	Zeremonie im Tower of London, bei der die Burg jede Nacht gesichert wird.
change *v* **hands**	den Besitzer wechseln
cheer *v* **(someone) up**	(jemanden) aufheitern
closet	(Wand)Schrank
clue	Hinweis, Indiz
cobbled	mit Kopfstein gepflastert
coincidence	Zufall
collide *v*	zusammenstoßen
commotion	Aufregung, Tumult, Aufruhr
companion	Begleiter(in)
compassionately	mitfühlend
confirm *v*	bestätigen
conspiratorially	verschwörerisch
copper *fam*	Bulle *fam,* Polizist
cover *v*	hier: berichten über; bedecken
crack *v* **up** *fam*	durchdrehen, zusammenbrechen
craftsmanship	Kunstfertigkeit
crisp	frisch; knusprig
crouch *v*	sich ducken, niederkauern

cry *v* **one's heart out** *fig*	sich die Seele aus dem Leib weinen *fig*
dab *v*	abtupfen
dashboard	Armaturenbrett
deceive *v*	betrügen, täuschen
decline *v*	hier: ablehnen; weniger werden
deliberately	absichtlich
demanding	anspruchsvoll
detest *v*	verabscheuen
devastated	hier: am Boden zerstört; verwüstet
disapproving	missbilligend
distinctive	charakteristisch, markant
distracted	abgelenkt
distressed	bekümmert, verzweifelt
dodge *v*	(schnell) ausweichen
dome	Kuppel
dreadful	furchtbar
drunk	Betrunkene(r)
dumbfounded	sprachlos, verblüfft
duster	Staublappen
eager	begierig, eifrig
emblazoned	geschmückt, verziert
enraged	wütend, aufgebracht
equipped	ausgerüstet
eternal	ewig, immerwährend
evidence	Beweis(e); Anhaltspunkt
evidently	augenscheinlich, offenkundig
fade *v*	hier: verschwinden; verblassen
faint *v*	ohnmächtig werden
fake	falsch, nachgemacht
far-fetched	weit hergeholt
fast-forward *v*	vorspulen
firm	bestimmt; fest

flash	Blitz(licht)
flash *v*	blitzen, blinken
flick *v* **through**	durchblättern
flinch *v*	zurückweichen, (zurück)zucken
flirtatious	kokett, flirtend
float *v*	treiben, schwimmen
fodder	Futter
footage	Filmmaterial
foot guard	Wächter zu Fuß
frantically	verzweifelt
frown *v*	die Stirn runzeln; finster schauen
fumble *v*	herumtasten
funeral	Beerdigung
furious	wütend; wild
fuss	Wirbel, Getue
gambling debts *pl*	Spielschulden
gasp *v*	keuchen
gem	Edelstein
get (got, got) *v* **rid of**	loswerden
get (got, got) *v* **round to something**	dazu kommen, etwas zu tun
give (gave, given) *v* **way**	nachgeben; ausweichen
glance *v*	blicken, den Blick werfen auf
glimpse	flüchtiger Blick
gloomily	düster, finster
go (went, gone) *v* **into hiding**	untertauchen
grab *v*	(zu)packen, schnappen
gracefully	anmutig
grand entrance *fig*	großer Auftritt *fig*
greed	Gier
grimly	grimmig, streng
grip	Griff; Halt
grunt *v*	hier: brummeln; grunzen

hand v	geben, reichen
handkerchief	Taschentuch
harm	Leid, Schaden
head v **back**	umkehren, zurückgehen
head v **for**	zusteuern auf
headline	Schlagzeile
headquarters	Hauptquartier
hiding place	Versteck
hiss v	fauchen, zischen
Home Secretary	Innenminister (UK)
honourable	ehrenwert, ehrenhaft
illuminate v	erleuchten, erhellen
impressive	beeindruckend
incredible	unglaublich
incredulously	ungläubig, skeptisch
inhale v	einatmen
in no time	im Nu
inquire v	nachfragen, sich erkundigen
insert v	einfügen
inspect v	untersuchen
instantly	sofort, unverzüglich
interior	das Innere; Innen...
interrogation	Verhör, Befragung
intervene v	einschreiten, eingreifen
in the picture *fig*	im Bilde *fig*
intimidated	eingeschüchtert
intruder	Eindringling
investigator	Ermittler(in)
invisible	unsichtbar
It's all right for some.	Manche haben's wirklich gut.
joyride	Spritztour
jump v **out of one's skin** *fig*	aus der Haut fahren *fig*
jump v **to conclusions**	voreilige Schlüsse ziehen

keen on	erpicht auf, stark interessiert an
Keep me posted!	Halt mich auf dem Laufenden!
lantern	Laterne
late	hier: jüngst verstorben; spät
lead	Spur, Fährte
leak *v*	durchsickern, auslaufen; tropfen
maiden name	Mädchenname
make (made, made) *v* **one's way**	sich auf den Weg machen, sich begeben
mankind	Menschheit
mantelpiece	Kaminsims
martial arts *pl*	Kampfsportarten
marvel *v* **(at)**	staunen (über)
mate *fam*	Kumpel, Kamerad, Gefährte
matter-of-factly	nüchtern, sachlich
merchandise	Ware(n)
mercy	Gnade
minor	gering, geringer
misfortune	Unglück
moan *v*	stöhnen, jammern
moat	Burggraben
mock *v*	verhöhnen, verspotten
mockingly	höhnisch, spöttisch
motionless	regungslos, bewegungslos
moustache	Schnurrbart
mumble *v*	nuscheln, murmeln
narrow-shouldered	mit schmalen Schultern
nave	Kirchenschiff
neatly	ordentlich; gewandt; treffend
nope *fam*	nö *fam*, nein
nothing (in) particular	nichts Besonderes
oak	Eiche
objection	Ablehnung; Einwand

observation wheel	Riesenrad
odd	hier: übrig; ungerade; merkwürdig
on duty	Dienst haben, im Dienst
outrage	Empörung, Entrüstung; Skandal
outshine, outshone, outshone *v, fig*	übertreffen, in den Schatten stellen *fig*
outskirts *pl*	Stadtrand; Außenbezirke
overhear, overheard, overheard *v*	zufällig (mit)hören
owe *v*	schulden; verdanken
palm	Handfläche; Palme
paramedic	Sanitäter(in)
pat *v*	klapsen, tätscheln
pensively	nachdenklich
philistine	Banause/Banausin
piercing	durchdringend, stechend
pillar	Säule
play *v* **(it) safe**	auf Nummer sicher gehen *fam*
plead *v*	flehen, bitten
pop *v*	knallen; stecken *fam*
posh *fam*	vornehm, piekfein *fam*
praise *v*	loben
precious	kostbar
premises *pl*	Gelände, Anwesen
pressure	Druck
pretend *v*	so tun als ob; vorgeben
proceed *v*	weitergehen; fortschreiten
prop *v* **up**	aufrichten
public parking facility	öffentliche Parkmöglichkeit
pull *v* **(something) off** *fam*	(etwas) durchziehen, abziehen *fam*
puzzled	verdutzt, verblüfft
Queen's Keys	Schlüssel für die Burgtore des Towers of London

rack *v*	quälen
rear-view mirror	Rückspiegel
reassuringly	beruhigend, unterstützend
recording	Aufnahme
regretfully	mit Bedauern, bedauernd
remorseful	reumütig
remote control	Fernbedienung
remotely	entfernt; fern
renowned (for)	berühmt (für), renommiert
reproachfully	vorwurfsvoll
reputation	Ruf, Ansehen
residential area	Wohngebiet
reverse	hier: Rückwärtsgang; Gegenteil
reward	Belohnung
rewind, rewound, rewound *v*	zurückspulen
riches *pl*	Reichtümer
ridiculous	lächerlich
rifle	Gewehr
rightful	rechtmäßig
roller-coaster	Achterbahn…, achterbahnmäßig
safety regulations *pl*	Sicherheitsbestimmungen
sardonically	höhnisch, süffisant
SAS (Special Air Service)	Spezialeinheit der britischen Armee
scarlet	scharlachrot
scent	Duft, Geruch
sceptre	Zepter
scoundrel	Schurke
scrutinize *v*	genau prüfen
sculptress	Bildhauerin
secretive	heimlich, verschwiegen
seemingly	scheinbar
see-through	durchsichtig

self-consciously	befangen; bewusst
sensation-craving	sensationslüstern
sentry, sentries *pl*	Wachen
set-up *fam*	abgekartetes Spiel *fam*; Falle
shaken	erschüttert, mitgenommen
shatter-proof	bruchsicher
shrug *v*	mit den Schultern zucken
shudder *v*	(er)schaudern
slippers *pl*	Hausschuhe
slumber	Schlummer, Nickerchen
slyly	schlau, verschlagen; hinterhältig
smash *v*	zerschmettern
smirk *v*	grinsen (hämisch)
snarl *v*	knurren; anfauchen
snatch *v*	schnappen; erhaschen
sneak *v* **up**	(sich) heranschleichen
snobbishness	Snobismus, Großspurigkeit
soothe *v* **(someone)**	(jemanden) beruhigen, trösten
sophisticated	elegant, gepflegt; kultiviert
spaceship	Raumschiff
sparkle *v*	funkeln
species	Lebensform, Spezies
spectator	Zuschauer(in)
speed *v*	rasen, schnell fahren
spellbound	fasziniert, verzaubert
spiritual justice	himmlische Gerechtigkeit
spread *v*	(sich) ausbreiten
square metre	Quadratmeter
squeal *v*	kreischen, schreien
stammer *v*	stammeln, stottern
start *v*	hier: zusammenzucken; starten
stately	würdevoll, stattlich
straight away	sofort

strike (struck, struck) *v* **(someone) down**	(jemanden) niederschlagen
striped	gestreift
stroke *v*	streicheln
stroll *v*	schlendern, bummeln
stubborn	stur, störrisch
stun *v*	betäuben
sulk *v*	schmollen
superior	Vorgesetzte(r)
superstitious	abergläubisch
suspect	Verdächtige(r)
swallow *v*	(ver)schlucken
swiftly	eilig
switch	Schalter
swollen	geschwollen
sword	Schwert
take (took, taken) *v* **hold of**	ergreifen
taken aback	erstaunt; betroffen
take (took, taken) *v* **to one's gun**	seine Waffe in Anschlag nehmen
teasingly	neckend, scherzend
temporal justice	weltliche Gerechtigkeit
terrifying	entsetzlich, erschreckend
tiptoe *v*	auf Zehenspitzen schleichen
toot	tuten, hupen
topple *v* **over**	umkippen, umfallen
tow *v*	(ab)schleppen
Traitor's Gate	„Verrätertor", ein Eingangstor zum Tower of London
tranquillizer	Beruhigungsmittel
treasure	Schatz
trespassing	unbefugtes Betreten
trickle *v*	sickern, rieseln, rinnen

trigger	Abzug (Waffe)
trimming	Dekoration; Besatz
trophy	Trophäe
tube *fam*	die Londoner U-Bahn; Röhre
tug *v*	ziehen
tut *v*	sich mokieren
typewriter	Schreibmaschine
unconscious	bewusstlos
under one's breath	im Flüsterton, flüsternd
unreliable	unzuverlässig
unsteady	unsicher, wackelig
upmarket	gehoben, vornehm
valuable	wertvoll
vanish *v*	verschwinden
vast	enorm, gewaltig
velvet	Samt
Victorian	viktorianisch, aus dem 19ten Jahrhundert
vital	hier: entscheidend; lebenswichtig
voice modifier	Stimmenwandler
waste of time	Zeitverschwendung
wearily	müde, resigniert
whilst	solange, während
whistle *v*	pfeifen
wickedly	boshaft, bösartig
wimp *fam*	Schwächling, Weichei *fam*
wink *v*	zwinkern
wisely	klugerweise
witness	Zeuge/Zeugin
worked up	aufgeregt
wrongful	unrechtmäßig
yawn *v*	gähnen
Yeoman Warder	Wärter im Tower of London

Compact Lernkrimis – Spannend Sprachen lernen

In der erfolgreichen Reihe sind erhältlich

- Compact Lernkrimis
- Compact Schüler-Lernkrimis
- Compact Lernkrimis History
- Compact Lernkrimi Kurzkrimis
- Compact Lernthriller
- Compact Lernstories Mystery
- Compact Lernkrimi Sprachkurse
- Compact Lernkrimi Hörbücher
- Compact Lernkrimi Audio-Learning

Sprachen	Lernziele
■ Englisch, American English, Business English	■ Grundwortschatz
■ Französisch	■ Aufbauwortschatz
■ Spanisch	■ Grammatik
■ Italienisch	■ Konversation
■ Deutsch als Fremdsprache	

Weitere Informationen unter
www.lernkrimi.de